A HISTORICAL NARRATIVE OF
IMAM ALI IBN ABI TALIB

ALI

THE ELIXIR OF LOVE

JALAL MOUGHANIA

Ali, The Elixir of Love

Author: Jalal Moughania

© 2021 The Mainstay Foundation

Calligraphy cover design: Zuhair Hussaini

Printed in the United States.

ISBN: 978-1943393060

To the Beloved of God, Muhammad.

CONTENTS

ARABIC SPELLING AND USAGE NOTE

In writing this book, I have elected to use more familiar English spellings for names of figures and subjects and have done so without diacritical marks. Thus, you will see Ali in-stead of 'Ali and Umar instead of 'Umar.

In addition, for the sake of fluidity, I have limited the use of honorary titles for the Holy Prophet Muhammad and his House-hold, such as Lady Fatima and Imam Ali, peace be upon them all. Therefore, you will see that most of the text will refer to them simply by their first name: Muhammad, Ali, Fatima, etc.

I have also limited the use of their full names, such as Ali ibn Abi Talib and Fatima bint Muhammad, to avoid the "Russian novel effect," keeping in mind the English reader who may be more easily confused with multiple unfamiliar names.

Furthermore, though "Koran" is often used in English works, I have elected to use the more proper spelling of "Quran" to differentiate between the *qaf* and *kaf* in the Arabic, which, if confused, could render different meanings of the word.

The reader should note that the supplication of *salawat* (a prayer asking God to send his peace and blessings upon Muhammad and the household of Muhammad) and salutations (peace be upon them) are usually recited at the mention of the Holy Prophet and his family. This is normally marked in elaborate calligraphy in Arabic text, or with (s), (a), or a similar mark in English text. Such marks do not appear in this book, so as not to disturb the flow of the reader. Nonetheless, the reader is encouraged to recite such prayers in their honor for the blessings of their mentioning.

It is worthy of note that I also relied on the English translation of Ali Quli Qara'i when citing the verses of the Holy Quran throughout this book, with minor adaptations. Moreover, I have italicized Arabic words, other than the names of individuals, when they first appear in the book.

I pray that these choices make the book more reader friendly to the intended audience, the English-speaking reader.

PREFACE

I remember the first time I visited the luminous shrine of Imam Ali in the holy city of Najaf, Iraq. It was July of 2010. I traveled with my brother, Ali, who had just graduated from the University of Michigan as a chemical engineer and many presumed was medical school bound with a second full-ride scholarship offer. To their surprise, but not mine, he had other plans. Ali decided to leave Ann Arbor, MI and move to Najaf to pursue seminary studies instead. Our visit, or *Ziyara*, in July, was in some ways Ali's introduction to his new home. I was blessed to experience that with him. He moved to Najaf months later and would reside near the shrine of Imam Ali for about five years.

Ali may not acknowledge this, because of his humility, but he has always been an inspiration for me in any work I put forth in the name of Ali ibn Abi Talib. Ali was the first "Ali" I knew. He was my older brother and I looked up to him. As a youth, he brought me, and the rest of our family in fact, closer to God. Coming to faith was, without a doubt, through falling in love with the personality of Imam Ali – the champion and hero of Islam.

As adults, I would joke and say that I wish I was named "Ali" – because how much I loved and admired the Imam. What an honor to be named after your hero, right? Nevertheless, I am glad my parents chose my brother for the name instead – he much better fit the part. I had my brother Ali as my example growing up, and as a personal mentor and teacher throughout adulthood. I owe him, amongst other mentors and teachers, for my admiration and love of Ali ibn Abi Talib.

Much of the inspiration behind this work has come from a deep admiration for the person of Ali – particularly his ability to leave a person from any walk of life forever touched. For much of my life, he has been the focal point of my identity and my reference in times of hardship and ease. The concept of "paying back" the one you are indebted to cannot be fathomed with Ali. You simply cannot pay him back. He has given us too much in light and virtue to calculate a repayment. The only solace I have is being encompassed by God's graces through Ali, and radiating that love into the world.

In writing this book, my intention was to highlight some of the most significant points in Imam Ali's life through insightful story telling. It starts before he was born with the settings of his grandfather, Abd al-Muttalib, and ends with Ali's dying wishes to his eldest son, Hasan. Though this is not purely a historical narrative, the work attempts to characterize itself with the genre without losing some analytical insight I felt to be important for the reader. Thus, you will see longer quotes, some monologues, and parts that aim to give deeper insight into the mind and soul of Ali. I hope that this work captures glimpses of the magnanimous life that Ali lived. Though thousands of pages could be written about the life and legacy of Ali, I preferred brevity manifested in these pages with the hopes of joining this work with ones similar to it on each of the members of Ali's household: his wife, Lady Fatima, his sons, Hasan and Husain, and his brother and master, Muhammad.

The primary source that I used for this historical narrative was the work of the late Sayyid Muhammad Bahreluloum *"Fi Rihab A'immat Ahlulbayt: Al-Imam Ameer al-Mu'mineen Ali"*. This original Arabic work is rich with a heavily researched narrative and well-cited insight into the life of Imam Ali. May the late Sayyid be rewarded immensely for his scholarly contributions through that book, which I have tremendously benefited from, as well as his many other works on Islamic history and thought.

The purpose of this historical narrative is to provide the English reader ease of access to the life and legacy of Ali. His life has tremendous lessons and moves us beyond inspiration and motivation – it is a lighthouse, captivating and guiding us through every new story in our own lives. His unwavering commitment to the brotherhood of man, the sanctity of faith, and the love of God, shows us the meaning of life. Ali moves us closer to our truest and highest selves.

From a socio-political context, Ali is often compared to his adversaries or challengers – the likes of Muawiya and the caliphs who ruled the Muslim nation before him. Ali's story should show that such comparisons are futile and out of touch. His position amongst men, and in the eyes of his Lord, was far beyond his contemporaries. There was no comparison for the charismatic leader, eloquent scholar, heroic warrior, and immaculate saint that was Ali.

I pray that the reader falls in love with Ali, as millions have across time, place, and creed. I pray that such a love illuminates your heart and opens your mind to what a life truly worth living actually looks like. To be Ali is far from me, but to be a mouthpiece for his legacy is the greatest honor I could long for. Please read each chapter with the intention of embracing truth, because that is what Ali is – Truth. As the Holy Prophet once said, "Ali is with the Truth, and the Truth is with Ali… it turns wherever he turns."

Though many in my circles growing up referred to Ziyara as a once-in-a-lifetime experience, I never looked at it that way. In 2010, I knew I would be back. In 2015, I visited twice in the same year. I would return to Najaf every year after that for Ziyara (up until the COVID-19 pandemic). Though brief, my trips were rejuvenating each and every time – as if coming to life, an elixir experienced in being the guest of Ali.

I took the opportunity to write parts of this work during some of those visits – asking the universe to assist me in finding the words that may do justice to his story. Speaking of the universe, I leave you with a gem of a saying from Ali – one that may take several lifetimes of reflection to fully embrace. A gift from the most gracious Prince Ali:

Your cure is within you, yet you do not sense it. Your sickness if rom you, yet you do not see it. You are the 'Clarifying Book' through whose letter becomes manifest the hidden. You presume you are insignificant, while within you lies the greater universe. You would not need what is outside of you, if only you would reflect….

I pray that the blessings of Imam Ali's resting place extend to the words on these papers, and to the eternal and resplendent souls of their readers. I pray the reader is inspired by the life and legacy of Ali, to understand him for what he truly is. The majestic gateway of knowledge, the immaculate path of deliverance, and the elixir of God's eternal Love... Ali.

CHAPTER 1

THE GUARDIAN OF GOD'S HOUSE

This house has a Lord who protects it.

– Abd al-Muttalib

The nights of Arabia were dark, yet majestic. The desert's sky was painted with its endless stars. They twinkled on the dark canvas as the admirers of the heavens looked up from below. It seemed as if the stars shined brightest for the knights of Banu Hashim, the noblest clan of Quraysh. The tribe of Quraysh itself was one of the most respected and powerful in Arabia. In those majestic nights, Banu Hashim gathered around their chief – a man who possessed a stature that very few in history were blessed with having. He stood tall, yet humble, wise, yet youthful, and strong, yet gentle. Their leader, their guardian, their protector was Abd al-Muttalib.

In the sixth century, Abd al-Muttalib walked amongst the Arabians as a royal prince whose mere presence demanded respect from all. His loyalty and nobility were unmatched. He had a place in the hearts of Arabians that no one else had. His love and dedication for his family was so unique, it drew admiration from all those around him. But his family was not limited to his clansmen: it encompassed all those who crossed his path. Nor was the place he called "home" confined to the valleys of Mecca: his home was rather all that he saw of God's Earth.

Two centuries later, one of his descendants would describe him by saying that, "God will bring forth Abd al-Muttalib on the Day of Judgment, and he will have the countenance of the prophets and the glory of kings."

Though the era he lived in was filled with paganism and the worship of countless idols, he never bowed before anything but the One. His heart was filled with faith and piety. People knew him as such, and even though they lived differently than he did and worshipped differently than he, they loved him and respected him. They believed in him and trusted in him.

One season, Mecca experienced a severe drought. The people prayed to their idols for days and weeks to change their situation, to bring down some water from the heavens to the scorching earth they wandered. But to no avail. They benefited nothing from the bowing and kneeling before the statues they called gods. Doubting whether their gods even heard their prayers, they beseeched a man who prayed to a god they did not see. They turned to Abd al-Muttalib. Perhaps he had an ability that they and their gods did not have. The people came to him and he humbly answered their pleas.

Abd al-Muttalib went out to the desert to pray to his lord under the open sky. Under the scorching sun, scores of people trailed behind him. They watched his every step, wondering if he could save them from the unforgiving drought of Arabia. He slowly raised his two hands to the heavens and began his prayer. Uttering words with complete focus and purpose, the people saw that he not only knew what to ask for, but that he meant every word to a true Divine Witness.

"My Lord, the Creator of the Universe, these people are your servants, and the children of your servants, and you see what has befallen us. Have us be rid of this drought and bring forth the rain…"

His simple words and soft prayers were repeated by his family members around him. After moments, he slowed his prayer and brought his voice to a whisper, almost to a complete silence. And then they felt it. A drop, then two, then countless. The clouds gathered across the big blue sky and blocked out the sun. Before they knew it, the desert was soaking with their prayer's rain. Some immediately rejoiced and danced under the rain, while others stood in disbelief, taking a moment to process what had just happened. Shaking each other with joyous embraces and laughter, soon they all frolicked and twirled under the heaven's showers. An hour before, they had faced the looming thought of death, and now they celebrated a new life through the prayers of Abd al-Muttalib.

The stories of his greatness are many, but perhaps the most amazing of them all came when he stood up to the army of Abraha in 570 AD. Abraha was an army general under the King-dom of Aksum, an ancient Habesha kingdom that controlled what are now Eritrea, Ethiopia, Eastern Sudan and Southern Yemen. Abraha became the governor of Himyar, a province of Yemen and a significant region of the Aksum Kingdom. Abraha eventually declared himself independent of Aksum and established himself as King of Himyar.

Wanting to expand his dominion and influence, Abraha built a grand cathedral in Yemen to be a center of worship and pilgrimage for the region. He aspired to attract Christians and non-Christians alike. He had competition, however. The Kaaba of Mecca reigned, even before Islam, as the center of pilgrimage for the people of Arabia. The Arabians, especially the tribe of Quraysh, were not interested in Abraha's cathedral, no matter how grand it was.

The Kaaba was their home and they saw no alternative to it. Seeing this as a hinderance to his ambitions of expansion, Abraha decided to lead an army into Arabia to demolish the Kaaba. With the destruction of their temple, the Arabs' faith would be demoralized and they would be forced to see the superiority of the Abraha's empire and its church.

History tells that Abraha's army of thousands marched on to Mecca with war-elephants, brought to Arabia from Abyssinia. The mere sight of their infantry, cavalry, and tank-like elephants struck fear in the hearts of the Meccans. The people panicked and headed for the hills. When the Meccans fled the city to save their lives, Abd al-Muttalib would remain. He was relentless in his loyalty to the house of God. His confidence was not in his own mortal might: it was in something greater. He held on to the walls of the Kaaba and looked up to the heavens as he had done so many times before.

He whispered, "My Lord, this is your house and these are your servants... protect them." His confidence was derived from that prayer.

As the forces of Abraha rolled through Mecca, it was as if the city was already theirs. Their commanders came closer to the city center, finally arriving at Abd al-Muttalib. "What say you?" Essentially they were asking him, "What do you really think is going to happen here, other than destruction of this house you wish to protect?"

Unmoved and unwavering, Abd al-Muttalib stayed his ground. In a few words he responded calmly and with conviction, "This house has a Lord who protects it."

Abraha's army advanced, but something was wrong. Their tanks, the elephants, were not moving. The men whipped the beasts, but they would not budge. Ropes were placed around the elephants' massive bodies and dozens of men pulled with all their might, but the elephants would not move. Within moments, as the men were busy trying to mobilize the once-tamed beasts, the sky grew dark. Arabia did not experience such sudden clouds of storm, so what blackened the sky in the midst of day?

Swarms of birds, unlike any kind they had ever seen, filled the desert sky. Thousands of birds soared above the men, filling their hearts with fear as their ears pierced with the echoes of their dreadful shrieks. Just as they entered fear in the hearts of the Meccans moments ago, rolling into the city with their heads high, Abraha's men were now distraught and panicked.

Abd al-Muttalib's prayers were answered. These birds were sent from the heavens, but to Abraha's army they were far from heavenly. The army of birds dropped tiny pebbles on the ground troops below. The altitude at which the birds flew and released these pebbles gave them such intensity that some described them as "fireballs from heaven."

Truth be told, Abraha's army was shattered within minutes. The pebbles pierced through the men and the beasts, leaving none standing but one man. One man who stood before the gate of the Kaaba and swore to protect it from harm. One man that believed in a cause greater than himself. One man whose faith was stronger than that of a nation. That man was Abd al-Muttalib – the trustee of his Lord and guardian of His house.

History would record 570 AD as the Year of the Elephant, after the triumph of Abd al-Muttalib over Abraha's army of beasts. This year was not only marked by triumph for the family of Abd al-Muttalib. It was also one of celebration, grief, and hope. In that year, Abd al-Muttalib celebrated the wedding of his beloved son, Abdullah. Abdullah was a tall, handsome, intelligent young man. He would be married to the graceful Amina bint Wahab, also from the tribe of Quraysh. The merry celebrations would come to a stop, however, with the unexpected death of Abdullah.

As he embarked on a business trip in Syria a few months after his wedding, Abdullah fell ill on the journey. He tragically passed away at the young age of twenty-five. His death left his father heartbroken. His bride, Amina, was shattered. He left behind some form of solace for his family, however. Amina was pregnant, expecting a son within a few short months. That son would be the great hope for the family of Abd al-Muttalib, and later for all humanity. The son's name would be *Muhammad.*

Abd al-Muttalib raised his sons with the same dedication and loyalty to God that he was praised for. After he passed, his son, Abd Manaf, later to be known as Abu Talib, would take his place in being that trusted believer of Quraysh and custodian of God's house. The tribe of Quraysh was certainly one of the largest and most influential tribes in Arabia. Not all were believers though. Some were pagan, some faithful, and some indifferent. But it was this tribe that would behold some of the most immaculate men and women the world would see. Abu Talib was surely one of them. For where would one go if he had a need or request of any sort, other than to the welcoming home of Abu Talib?

Abu Talib became his father's reflection, after having been his shadow for so many years. It was a pursuit of his to honor Abd al-Muttalib's deep tradition of generosity, valor, and service. And with all this nobility, he would crown it with faith. Like his father, he believed in the immaculate oneness of God and prostrated only to Him. His lineage would pride themselves on doing the same.

CHAPTER 2

A LEGEND IS BORN

Ali was the most beloved to Muhammad...

– Al-Abbas ibn Abd al-Muttalib

The knights of Banu Hashim would come together for a glorious night. The family gathered joyously. The men, the women, and the children sat around in a circle near the Kaaba – the house of God they protected. As with any family gathering, conversations ensued, jokes were made, and laughter broke out within the smaller circles of the family. But as their chief approached, the chatter gave way to silence. The weight of his prestige was felt in every step he took. The laughter would cease, and the stillness would follow. His family did not fear him: they were in awe of him. They admired Abd al-Muttalib and endeared him. Even if he was just gone for a short while, his children and grandchildren longed for him. He was the father of them all.

Abd al-Muttalib walked into the family's circle and the youngsters quickly cleared multiple seats for him to take his place. Wherever he would sit, that space would become the focal point of the gathering. He smiled graciously and slowly sat down. Twinkles in their eyes, they gazed at their gallant father, waiting for him to speak.

Looking towards his son, Abu Talib, he said, "Is it not time for you to get married, and for us to celebrate your marriage, my son?"

Abu Talib's eyes, however, were glued to the ground. A moment of silence passed. The bashful son mustered the courage to respond without moving his gaze from the sand at his feet,

"You are better to assess the interests of your children, O' father..."

Abd al-Muttalib smiled, "And do you have a liking of any of the daughters of Arabia?"

"No father... whatever you choose, for that is what I would have comfort and contentment in."

The silence grew louder.

The family glanced back and forth at the bashful son and the endeared father. Not much time passed, but to those in the gathering, time could not have gone by any slower. Who would Abd al-Muttalib choose for his son? The choice was not an easy one.

The Banu Hashim were viewed as royalty amongst the Arabians, uniquely standing out from within their tribe of Quraysh. As such, any home in Arabia would proudly see their daughter be wed to the young Abu Talib. Such homes raised daughters that Banu Hashim would be proud to take in as their own. So, the choice was even more difficult and time felt like eternity.

While Abu Talib's bashful eyes fixated on the sand, Abd al-Muttalib's gaze did not leave his son. He was proud of the man

his son had become. The respect and honor reflected in his mannerisms were not a show of weakness or incompetence, but rather of humility and humbleness. Abd al-Muttalib stroked his
grey beard and smiled. That smile lit up that dark night like a
flaming lantern in a Meccan cave.

"O' Abd Manaf, I have chosen for you Fatima, the daughter
of my brother, Asad. I pray that you are happy with my
choice…"

Everyone smiled joyously, including Abu Talib. There could
not have been a better choice. The young couple would grow to
build one of the purest homes of Arabia. Abu Talib and Fatima
were faithful, generous, and brilliant. It was their humble home
that raised a young orphan boy… a boy who would grow up to
be the greatest man to walk this Earth – Muhammad.

Indeed, Abu Talib and Fatima raised the Prophet Muhammad in their home. Muhammad was Abu Talib's nephew, the
son of his brother, Abdullah. As told, Muhammad's father
passed away months before he was born. His mother, Amina,
would care for him as mother and father. Her love was all-en-
compassing. But within a few short years, she too would pass
away, leaving Muhammad orphaned of mother and father. He
was six years old.

For two years after the passing of his mother, Muhammad
would grow under the care of his grandfather, Abd al-Muttalib.
He loved Muhammad dearly. He was the center of his universe.
Abd al-Muttalib took his grandson wherever he went. They
walked the desert and reflected on God's creation. The vastness

of the blue sky could not be rationed. The grains of the golden sand could not be tallied. The favors of God could not be numbered. Such reflections carried on in the shadow of the Kaaba, a place they both loved to be. Abd al-Muttalib was the protector of that blessed house of God, and in due time his grandson would be too.

"Great things will come from you, my son," Abd al-Muttalib repeated to his grandson. Muhammad would look up at his loving grandfather and smile.

But Abd al-Muttalib would not stay forever. Muhammad would lose yet another beloved. Before he died at the age of eighty, Abd al-Muttalib assigned the responsibility of raising Muhammad to his son, Abu Talib. Abd al-Muttalib told Abu Talib, "This boy will be something great. Protect him. Do not let any harm come his way."

Surely, Abu Talib would do as his father wished. He would take in his young nephew and raise him like his own. His wife Fatima shared Abu Talib's empathy, compassion, and readiness to care for Muhammad.

The Archangel Gabriel would come to Muhammad later in life and tell him, "O' Muhammad, God sends you His peace and says, 'I have forbidden Hellfire on the backbone that begot you, the womb that held you, and the chest that embraced you...'"

He responded, "O' Gabriel, who are they?"

"The backbone that begot you is your father, Abdullah ibn Abd al-Muttalib, while the womb that held you is your mother,

Amina bint Wahab. And as for the chest that embraced you, it is Abd Manaf ibn Abd al-Muttalib and Fatima bint Asad."

Abd al-Muttalib tasked his son to protect that orphan. With the care of Abu Talib, that boy would grow to be the Mercy to Mankind. Every day that passed in his lifetime, Muhammad grew closer and closer to saving humanity from slavery and bondage, to freedom and honor. As a young man of his twenties, Muhammad was already seen as *Al-Sadiq* (The Truthful) and *Al-Ameen* (The Trusted) of his community. That was an honor for the house of Abu Talib. A gifted poet and orator, Abu Talib would later in life recite words of poetry describing his relationship to Muhammad:

> By my life, I am utterly devoted to Muhammad and his brethren, with all the devotion of a close admirer.

> He is kind, intelligent, just, steady, the ally of a God of whom he is ever aware.

> And the Lord of men has aided him with victory, and he has brought forth a religion the truth of which shall stay.

> I cared for him myself, protected him, and defended him by our heads and chests.

And there was more that came from the house of Abu Talib and Fatima… there was surely more.

It was a Friday morning and the thirteenth day of the month of Rajab. Muhammad was thirty years of age at that time. Abu Talib's wife, Fatima, was expecting another son. Three days prior to that Friday, she found herself circulating the Kaaba in worship. Fatima asked God for mercy and strength in her pregnancy. As she prayed, she felt a sharp pain – too similar to the pangs of labor. Some say that such laborious pain was not expected as she had yet to come full term in her pregnancy. As she contemplated the possibilities, she was interrupted again by the rippling pain. The pain overwhelmed Fatima and made it nearly impossible to contain her groans of agony.

Eyes turned to her and Fatima knew that it was time. But where would she go? The pangs of labor quickly paralyzed her, and she found herself unable to leave the Kaaba's holy site. Her palms clenched the skirts of the Kaaba and she held on to dear life. Not wanting to continue as a victim of people's unforgiving eyes, she took the cloth of God's House and covered herself with it.

She called out to the Heavens and said, "O' Lord of this house, veil me… and save me and my baby from every harm."

Her short prayer barely ended and the walls of the Kaaba began to crack. There was no earthquake felt for the walls to tremble, nor lightning to bring down its mighty walls. The walls of the Kaaba miraculously opened for her and she walked in. It was as if the angels of Heaven carved out an opening and welcomed the daughter of Asad into God's House. Protected she was, as her Lord veiled her from every harm. People stood in awe as they saw the Kaaba walls open up and close after her. They could no longer see nor hear Fatima. She was in the guardianship of the Kaaba's angels and no one else.

Abu Talib would come to the scene within the hour. One of the neighbors had recognized Fatima and quickly went to inform Abu Talib of his wife's labor. Abu Talib would patiently wait outside the walls of the Kaaba for the news of his newborn baby. Behind him was a crowd of Banu Hashim, anxiously awaiting their new baby cousin.

For three days, Fatima would stay within the walls of the Kaaba. Finally, as the fourth day broke, Fatima would come out. The walls of the Kaaba would open up once again for her grand exit. She held her baby boy, who was wrapped in the cloth of the Kaaba, and enjoyed the greatest smile, seen only on the face of a mother. Abu Talib leaped towards her in excitement. She handed her boy to his jubilant father.

Abu Talib held his son in his hands. He too smiled so brightly, the family behind the couple gleaming in joy. Given the distinguished honor of being born in the Kaaba itself, Abu Talib knew the perfect name for his newborn son.

"His name will be Ali," he said as he smiled down at his baby boy. The high, the elevated, the champion – Ali.

It was as if, with the birth of Ali, the Kaaba would experience a new era. This boy was special. No one had the honor that he just experienced. No one in history was, or would be, born in the Kaaba. No one. The family knew he was special, and that he was no ordinary boy. Amongst the family that day was Ali's cousin, Muhammad. An evident truth under the sun and skies, no one was happier that day than Muhammad. For on that day, it was not only his cousin that was born – it would be his best friend, his confidante, and his successor.

It is said that the first person the newborn Ali opened his eyes to was Muhammad. And from that day, Ali never did take his eyes off him.

Ali was born to amazing parents and surrounded by many siblings, three brothers and three sisters, who loved him and cared for him deeply. Though their home was a humble one, it never felt void or empty. When Ali was only five years old, however, Mecca was struck with a terrible famine.

Although Abu Talib was a wealthy, successful man, his family, like many families, suffered as well. The difference was that Abu Talib never turned anyone away; throughout the famine, he still welcomed guests into his home and cared for any needy person who knocked on his door. His generosity knew no bounds.

To ease the inevitable hardship that would ensue, some of Abu Talib's family members asked to care for his sons during the famine. The help came from Abu Talib's brothers, Hamza and Al-Abbas, as well as his nephew Muhammad. Abu Talib had four sons: Talib, Jafar, Aqeel, and Ali. Their relatives came over to pick up the sons of Abu Talib. It is said that their mother, Fatima, preferred to keep Aqeel with her, so he stayed home under her care. Talib would be taken under the wing of his uncle, Al-Abbas, and Hamza would care for Jafar.

Standing there as they were assigned, Muhammad would smile and say to the youngest of the brothers, "And I have chosen the one whom God has chosen for me." Ali smiled back at his cousin Muhammad.

Though the famine would pass, Ali would remain under the care of his beloved cousin Muhammad. Ali grew up in the household of Muhammad, just as Muhammad grew up in the household of Abu Talib. Muhammad would cook for him and feed him by his own hand as he sat in his lap. Ali followed his cousin wherever he went. Muhammad taught him all that he knew. Ali became his shadow.

He emulated every stroke and every move, every smile and every laugh. People were in awe of the maturity of this young man, as he was such an inspiring reflection of Muhammad's unmatched character and stature. The early companions of the Prophet would describe it by saying, "We used to look at Ali during the days of the Prophet, the same way we looked up at the stars in the sky…"

Ali himself would describe his childhood with the Prophet in saying, "I followed the Prophet wherever he went… every day he would teach me something new from the chest of his wisdom and ethics, and then he would order me to act on it."

Many years later, Fadl ibn Al-Abbas asked his father, who also happened to be Muhammad's uncle, "Who was the most beloved child to the Prophet?"

"Ali was the most beloved to him," Al-Abbas answered his son.

Confused, Fadl responded to this father, "Wait. I am asking you about his own children, who was the most beloved to him of his own children?"

"Ali was more beloved and adored to him than all of his children. He never spent a moment away from him, unless he absolutely had to travel for work. We never witnessed a father better to a son than he was to Ali, nor did we see a son who was more devoted to a father than Ali was to Muhammad..."

Muhammad raised Ali and shaped him to be the man he would become. Ali would become Muhammad's closest companion, confidante, and the gatekeeper to his true self. It is no surprise that the Prophet would say to his companions, "Ali is from me and I am from Ali, and he is the master of every believer after me."

CHAPTER 3

THE BLESSED UNION

If Ali was not created, there would be no match for Fatima.

– Muhammad

When he was a young man in his twenties, Muhammad found his heavenly match. Working with his uncle, Abu Talib, as a trader and merchant, Muhammad had gained a great reputation. He was praised for his intelligence, trustworthiness, and constancy. His ethics were unmatched. He was trusted by all. One day, Abu Talib was beseeched by Lady Khadija bint Khuwaylid. Khadija inherited her father's trading enterprise, one of the largest in Arabia, and was a distinguished businesswoman in her own right. She was highly respected and regarded across Arabia, with some even addressing her as the Princess of Quraysh. Khadija needed more trustworthy and dependable associates in her expanding enterprise, but had trouble finding them. She turned to Abu Talib, just as many in Quraysh had before her, asking if he could provide her with someone she could trust. Abu Talib knew the perfect man for the job.

Not much time passed, and Muhammad was representing Khadija's business enterprise in a trade journey in Syria. Therein Khadija's aides closely observed Muhammad and would report back to her. She knew of his stellar character, both from Abu Talib and the reputation Muhammad had earned across Arabia with the public. Still, she wanted to hear what he was like, directly from her closest aides.

"What did you learn about him?" Khadija asked her aide, Maysara, upon their return from Syria.

"He only eats once everyone else has. He is generous and kind, always truthful. He treats his subordinates with respect, and always carries a beautiful scent with him. And when he walks, it seems as if there is a cloud above him, following him wherever he goes."

Khadija's respect and admiration for Muhammad grew stronger. She came to see him not only as a trusted associate and agent, but as her potential life partner. Khadija did not delay and sent her marriage proposal to Muhammad. Simply, he saw her as she saw him – a perfect match. Muhammad was honored and accepted. With the blessings of his uncle, Abu Talib, the marriage took place and surely was a festive event for the whole of Mecca. Abu Talib stood before all the guests of the ceremony and delivered a sermon in honor of the graceful newlyweds:

All praise and glory be to God, the creator of Heavens and Earth, and thanks to him for all his blessings, bounties, and mercy. He sent us into this world as the heirs of Abraham and Ismael. He made us the guardians of his house, which is a sanctuary for all. My nephew, Muhammad ibn Abdullah ibn Abd al-Muttalib is unmatched in wisdom and intelligence, in purity of lineage and family distinction. He has all the markings of a man destined to be great. He is marrying Khadija, the daughter of Khuwaylid. May God bless them both and protect them.

It truly was a match made in heaven. Muhammad and Khadija would build the most beautiful home. It was in their home that the young Ali was raised. Together, the loyal Ali and the faithful Khadija would be the first to believe in Muhammad's prophetic mission. Khadija was the first Muslim to accept the message of Muhammad. She did so willingly, genuinely, and without hesitation. The Prophet described his love for Khadija and her unconditional support for him:

I was invigorated by her love… She believed in me when no one else did; she accepted Islam when people rejected me; and she helped and comforted me when there was no one else to lend me a helping hand. God gave me children only through Khadija.

It was in her home that Muhammad's only daughter would be born – the Lady of Light – Fatima. The young Fatima would be praised by her father as one of the four best women to have ever come and that would ever be. The others were Asiya (the pious wife of Pharaoh), Mary (the mother of Jesus), and of course, her mother, Khadija. Fatima was the foremost of these immaculate women. *Sayyidat Nisa al-Alameen* – the Leader of the Women of the Worlds.

Years later, when Muhammad's beloved daughter, Fatima, would come of age, the suitors that knocked on their door to ask for her hand were too many to count. They all desired to hold the honor of being the Prophet's son-in-law of course, but more so the honor of being wed to the Lady of Light. Many came forward and offered the bounties of this world, but none of it moved the Prophet from his firm position. To each that would knock, he would reply, "Wait for what is decided."

This, nonetheless, did not deter more from knocking. The more that knocked, the more left disappointed. Each thought that they had something better or more special to offer. But to the House of the Prophet, they were all the same. None of them were the one. The whole ordeal became tiresome to the Prophet. When people persistently asked him about what was going on, if a suitor were to be chosen for Fatima, he insisted that they should not bring up the matter to him anymore.

Ali was a witness to this. He had grown in the Prophet's home and become a complete individual in his own right. His parents had both passed, and he was ready to build a family of his own. Who better of a partner for Ali than Fatima? But Ali decided to avoid the situation. He heard of all the things these suitors came with, and the assurances of wealth and social prominence. He surely did not have those things. Ali was young, humble, and far from extravagant. Thus, for a while, he waited patiently and accepted that hopes may only be dreams.

Back to the many suitors - well, they only grew more frustrated. Practically every possible suitor knocked on the Prophet's door, and they all were turned away. The only person who did not knock and attempt to ask for Fatima's hand was Ali.

"Let Ali be like us, let him ask so that he may be rejected like we were," some would exclaim. Validating their own shortcomings may have been what they desired, but people should be careful of what they wish for.

A group of failed suitors came to Ali and pushed him towards asking for Fatima's hand. They urged him to go forward with it and not to hesitate.

But Ali thought about it long and hard. After all, he was very close to the Prophet. He grew up in his home and was raised by him. The Prophet knew him better than anyone else, and the qualities he developed as a young man were thanks to the Prophet's example. But he heard it from the Prophet more than once: "Wait for what is decided."

At the same time, the Prophet continued to insist that he did not want this subject brought up to him anymore. So, what would his answer be to him if he were to come forward? More crucially, getting married requires assets. All Ali owned in this world was his sword, his shield, and nothing else. So, how could he get married, especially when Fatima was promised a dowry that could fill the valleys of Mecca with gold and silver?

But the more he thought about it, the more resolute he became in going forward. He realized all these limitations, but they did not stop him. No matter what it would cost him, he would do whatever it took to make this work. If Muhammad were to accept him in this matter, he would figure out a way forward.

And thus, Ali walked to the house of Muhammad as he fought off his bashfulness and all the thoughts that overwhelmed him.

People watched him take that long walk to the Prophet's house. His steps were heavy and slow, his hesitation definitely apparent. It appeared as if he was not the war hero that everyone knew him as. It was not the champion of the battlefield walking this dirt road. Though chatter surrounded him, and the eyes closed in on him, he was not distracted. His thoughts were consumed by "the ask" he was going to make. He was about to ask for the hand of the most pristine young lady of Arabia, that the world had ever witnessed, for that matter.

People gathered to see how Ali would be greeted by the Prophet. Would he be turned away like the rest? Or would the outcome be different? People argued amongst themselves and predictions filled the air. Some swore by everything that he would be rejected like everyone else was. Well, of course he would. He was, in their eyes, no more prominent than the likes of Abu Bakr and Umar; nor was he greater in stature and wealth than Uthman and Ibn Aouf – all of whom were seen as leading companions of the Prophet.

Some others, though, looked at it differently, and observed carefully. They said that this one may be different. He grew up in the same home as the Prophet and was seen by the Prophet in a different light than any of the Muhajiroun (those who migrated with the Prophet from Mecca to Medina) and Ansar (those who welcomed and supported the Prophet in the city of Medina). The few remembered the Prophet's words to his companions, "Loving Ali is a virtue that cannot be contradicted by a sin, and hating Ali is a sin that cannot be remedied by any good deed."

And so, Ali went forward, relying on God, and God alone. He made his way to his cousin's house. He arrived at the humble home and stood before its wooden door. As he raised his hand to knock on the door, he found his hand trembling. With his trembling hand, he created a fist, and with that fist he knocked. The Prophet knew that knock. He knew who was behind the door. A smile grew on his face.

"Um Salama, please open the door to the most beloved of God's creation to me..." Muhammad asked his wife.

Um Salama quickly got up, so interested to see who owned such a title. She looked through the cracks in the wooden door before opening it and saw that it was Ali.

"Of course," she thought to herself with a smile.

Who else would have such a place in the heart of Muhammad? Throughout her lifetime, Fatima watched as her father showered Ali with praise and adoration.

"Ali is my brother in this life and the hereafter... Ali is the Imam of the pious, the prince of believers, and the leader of the resplendent... Ali is with the Quran, and the Quran is with Ali..."

As Um Salama opened the door, the Prophet followed her and welcomed Ali with an embrace. Still, this visit was different than any visit Ali had made before. Even though he was raised in the Prophet's home, his tongue was tied by a bashfulness the Prophet had not seen before from Ali. The champion of every battle the Prophet faced, the warrior feared by all of Arabia, and the bravest commander his era had witnessed – in these moments was simply different.

Ali was surely nervous. Knowing Ali so well, the Prophet could tell. He smiled at his cousin. The son of Abu Talib was not only the bravest warrior of Arabia: he was an articulate scholar and amazing orator. He mesmerized people in gatherings with his eloquence. However, in those moments it was but a few words that were uttered from the lips of Ali.

The Prophet looked at his cousin and smiled. He knew what made him nervous. He knew why his demeanor was so different than it had ever been. To make it easier for Ali, who had not said anything but a few basic pleasantries since he walked in, the Prophet came closer to him.

"Tell me, O' Ali, what is in your heart?" the Prophet said.

Ali looked at the Prophet blankly and then to the ground. He did not answer. Sweat dripped down his forehead and he only grew more nervous.

The Prophet followed, "What is wrong Ali? Say what is in your heart."

Later in life, Ali would describe to one of his companions these moments.

He would say, "When I entered the Prophet's home and saw him, he had such a beautiful magnificence and prestige about him. I sat down with him and was completely overcome. By God, I could not utter a single word."

"You must have come to ask for Fatima's hand," the Prophet said to Ali.

"Yes," Ali managed to reply to his cousin.

"Marhaban wa Ahlan!" Welcome! Welcome! Muhammad replied to Ali, delighted.

The Prophet would leave the living room to speak to his daughter, Fatima, and ask her what she thought of the matter. As he approached Fatima, the young maiden sent from the heavens, he admired her grace and piety. He sat next to her and embraced her with his warmth. She smiled at her father, awaiting what news he came with.

"My dear, Ali is here. You know how close he is and the sacrifices he has made for our faith… and I have asked my Lord to wed you to the best of His creation, and the most beloved to Him…" he paused.

"Ali is asking for your hand," the Prophet said with his magnificent smile.

Fatima grew silent in bashfulness. Her cheeks reddened and she looked down to the floor with humbleness. He waited a moment. He knew what was in her heart and the contentment she had in his words. Fatima knew Ali better than anyone. She watched him as she grew up and saw his position with her father. She knew what he gave to Islam, and how he was seen in the eyes of their Lord.

Fatima saw that he was the complete human being, having adopted every virtue known to man. She was elated that Ali had asked for her, but her bashfulness quieted her, just as it silenced the eloquent champion, Ali. They both were humbled before the prestige of the Prophet. He understood them both just as much as he loved them.

The Prophet went back to the living room to give Ali the great news, and then made his way outside, where he found swarms of people waiting.

"Light has been paired with light! If it were not for Ali, there would be no match for my Fatima!"

Their wedding was like no other. Such a perfect union of celebration and faith, glory and humbleness, happiness and piety. The Prophet was so happy. The man who never wore anything but a smile was never seen as delighted as he was on the day of their wedding.

Abd al-Muttalib would wed his son, Abdallah, to Amina bint Wahab, to bear the fruit that would be Muhammad, the Messenger of God. He would then wed his son, Abu Talib to Fatima bint Asad, to bear the fruit that would be Ali, the guardian of God's Message. And now Muhammad would wed his daughter, Fatima to that Ali, and from their marriage would be born the eleven immaculate princes who would forever guard the faith for humankind.

The Prophet said, "I am the Principal of Prophets and Ali is the Master of Guardians, and the guardians after me are twelve.

The first of them is Ali ibn Abi Talib, and the last of them is the Mahdi…"

When Ali and Fatima got married, the Prophet made a prayer:

God, give blessings through them, send blessings upon them, and bless their progeny.

The virtues of Ali could not be counted. But we will see, as the story unfolds, why the greatest lady and daughter of Muhammad, Fatima, could only be matched with the greatest man after the Prophet – Ali.

CHAPTER 4

THE BROTHER OF THE PROPHET

O' Ali, you are my brother, my successor, my vicegerent, my heir, and my caliph after me.

– Muhammad

The love Ali had for God was unmatched. It was a love he experienced through Muhammad, *Habeeb Allah* – the Beloved of God. He was nurtured by him since the day he was born, and Ali turned to none but God:

I worshiped God for seven years before anyone of this nation came to faith. I heard the Voice and I saw the Light, while the Messenger of God had yet to proclaim his message to the world.

Ali was Muhammad's companion in faith and the brother he never had. As the brother of the Prophet, Ali followed his every footstep. The Prophet raised him with his immaculate inspiration, filling his heart with divine love. Ali's family saw it so clearly in him from a young age. Abu Talib would find the young Ali standing next to his cousin, Muhammad, in prayer. They were worshipping in one of the groves of Mecca, away from people's attention. Abu Talib looked on to his son and watched him move solemnly, kneeling, prostrating, and supplicating. When Ali completed his prayers, he turned to his side and found his father gazing upon him.

O' father, I believe in God and His messenger. I have faith in what he has come forth with and I have followed him.

Tears of joy ran down the cheeks of Abu Talib. What more can a father ask for? He would smile at his son and say, "O' Ali, as he will only call onto you for what is virtuous... hold on to him."

Abu Talib did not stop there. He called on his son, Jafar, and told him to join his brother and cousin in prayer. Ali was on the Prophet's right, so "join him on his left," Abu Talib said to Jafar. He told him not to miss this opportunity of honor to be of the first to enter this faith, and to hold onto to the rope of God, through Muhammad.

The early days of Islam were just like that. The Prophet had only a handful of followers, namely his cousin Ali and his beloved wife Khadija. Ali was the moon of their night, filling their home with life and joy. Ali was the light of their day, and the warm sun of their skies. Ali was... Ali.

When God ordered Muhammad to declare his message to the public and proclaim his prophethood to the world, He told him to make the proclamation to his family first:

Warn the nearest of your kinsfolk and lower your wing to the faithful who follow you. But if they disobey you, say, 'I am absolved of what you do.' And put your trust in the All-mighty, the All-merciful.

Thus, Muhammad invited all his relatives for a feast that would take place in the home of his uncle, Abu Talib. It is known as *Dawat al-Ashira*, or the Summoning of the Tribe. Muhammad tasked Ali to take care of all the arrangements –the food, the invitations, the setup, and everything in between – and the young Ali took care of it. Over forty men from the family would attend this feast. After their meal, Muhammad would address his uncles and relatives:

O Sons of Abd al-Muttalib! By God, I do not know of any person among the Arabs who has come to his people with better than what I have brought to you. I have brought to you the good of this world and the next, and I have been commanded by the Lord to call you unto Him....

The Prophet then paused. They waited for what he would say next.

Therefore, who amongst you will support me in this matter, so that he may be my brother, my successor, and my caliph among you?

They looked at Muhammad and then at one another, but no one responded. The silence only grew louder. But soon enough it would be broken.

"I will be your aid, O' Messenger of God," the young Ali would stand and proclaim.

Muhammad would smile and nod to Ali. He would repeat his words once more, asking his relatives who would take this opportunity with him. The silence was also repeated. To that, Ali would stand again and say, "I will be there to help you, O' Messenger of God!"

For a second time he would smile and nod to Ali. Muhammad would for a third time ask his family members the same question. "Who amongst you will support me in this matter so that he may be my brother, my successor, and my caliph among you?"

No response came from amongst them. But the young Ali would jump to his feet for a third time and say,

"I am your supporter, O' Messenger of God."

This young man filled the room with his confidence and faith, with his courage and servitude. When men five times his age could not form words to reply to Muhammad's request, he repeated his wholehearted belief three times. He did not care whether or not it had the approval of others; he knew it was truth, and he was committed to it.

Muhammad would smile and announce to the gathering as he replied to Ali's unwavering position of support.

O' Ali, you are my brother, my successor, my vicegerent, my heir, and my caliph after me....

At that statement, the men rose to their feet in a fit of anger and envy. They looked at Abu Talib with glaring eyes and mocked him. Abu Lahab, his brother, looked at him and said with the utmost mockery and sarcasm, "O' Abu Talib, congratulations to you on the day you enter the religion of your nephew, when he has made your youngest son a master over you!"

Ali was not pushed to stand up and proclaim his dedication to Muhammad just because he was his cousin. Everyone there was family. It was not because Ali had an emotional connection to his cousin either. In fact, everyone present was fond of Muhammad. Ali not only loved the Prophet, he saw him, even at such a young age, as the undeniable truth that must be followed in order to radiate the mercy of the Beloved Lord to mankind.

So, he rose up from the deep conviction he held in his heart to follow God. He was born in God's house. He never bowed before an idol a day in his life. The only god he knew was God. So, he followed his Prophet in every which way he could. He would do this knowing the consequences that could follow from the tribe of Quraysh. Ali knew that the pagans of Mecca were not easy foes. Still, he would rise up to the occasion, time and time again, to be the greatest companion, supporter, and brother to Muhammad.

CHAPTER 5

THANKS BE TO GOD

I give you my life, O' Messenger of God.

– Ali

Time passed and the movement of faith would only grow stronger. Islam was spreading across Arabia. Its message resonated with people and made a home in their hearts. Its impact and influence, however, began to threaten those in power. It just so happened to be that those who assumed power were too often those who discriminated and oppressed.

Islam would change that. In the eyes of God, there was no difference between black or white, Arab or Persian, rich or poor. The way of God saw no color. It only saw piety. Ali was the manifestation of such piety. But through that piety was the greatest courage the world would ever see. That courage laid his life on the line to protect the Messenger of God, time and time again.

When Abu Talib was still alive, the people of Quraysh thought twice before harassing Muhammad and his followers. Abu Talib was the protector and guardian of the Prophet. He considered him as one of his own sons, raised him in his home, and when Muhammad proclaimed his message, Abu Talib believed in him. So as long as Abu Talib was in the midst of Muhammad, no one would come near him.

In the end, Abu Talib was one of the elders of Quraysh, and was respected in every which way by the Arabs, especially those of Quraysh. But when Abu Talib's eyes forever closed and he went on to meet his Lord, the pagans of Quraysh became more daring. They came together and conspired to finally be rid of Muhammad and his new religion.

The meeting would take place in the home of Qusay ibn Kilab. There, the elders of Quraysh, men of reputation and thought, would come together and concoct their plans. This was the place from which any major event would be planned and decided for the tribe.

No man and woman from the tribe would be married outside of this home's decree. No declaration of war would be announced unless it came through here first. And no one under the age of forty was even allowed to step foot in this place to convene in the matters decided. From there, after Abu Talib's death, their hatred and animosity were evident; they no longer had the patience for the Prophet and his followers.

Muhammad and the Muslims were constantly attacked, such that the Prophet sent a group of Muslims to flee Mecca and take refuge in Abyssinia. The King of Abyssinia at that time was a pious Christian ruler who welcomed the Muslims and honored Muhammad.

The Prophet instructed his followers to show their hosts the greatest level of honor, appreciation and dignity. They were not there to preach, nor try to convert their hosts. Rather, they were to show them the highest regard and respect as guests in their lands.

While some of his companions had found haven in the lands of Abyssinia, the Prophet and the rest of his followers were still being persecuted in Mecca. In fact, there was an elaborate scheme underway to assassinate Muhammad once and for all. They plotted to take his life silently as he slept in his bed late at night, in the comfort of his home. But little did they know that the Prophet was aware of their schemes.

The Prophet had to act quickly, but not hastily. He decided that he would leave Mecca on that very night and escape to Medina incognito. No one was to be aware of his departure. However, the assassins were watching the home closely. They were set on killing Muhammad in his sleep that night. They had planned every detail and were adamant on executing their plan.

But if Muhammad was not home, then their plans would be spoiled, and they would need to quickly chase him down so that he could not get too far. The Prophet needed someone to take his place, in order to evade their detection. So, who would be the hero? Rather, who would be the sacrifice?

Who other than the son of Abu Talib would give himself without hesitation? Ali did not fear death and he especially did not waver from an opportunity to be of service and sacrifice to his prophet. When Muhammad proposed the idea to him, Ali's face lit up with the biggest smile.

He prostrated on the ground and said three times, "Thanks be to God."

He would rise to his feet with that same beautiful smile, look at his cousin and say, "O' Messenger of God, and with this will you be safe from evil and misfortune?"

"Yes, Ali."

"Then I give you my life, O' Messenger of God."

Mind you, this was not the first time that Ali would risk his life for the Prophet. While Abu Talib was still alive, during the first years of Muhammad's proclamation of Islam, Abu Talib would ask Muhammad to stay with him in his home most nights. He feared that the pagans of Quraysh would take his life, but so long as he was within Abu Talib's purview, they would not dare.

Still, Abu Talib would take additional measures to safeguard his nephew, Muhammad. He would have his son, Ali, alternate on some of the nights to sleep where Muhammad usually slept, in case they had the audacity to attack Muhammad in Abu Talib's home. Ali was ready to give his life for Muhammad on any given night.

As promised, Ali took the Prophet's place on that dry summer Meccan night. He would sleep in his bed as the Prophet would slip into the darkness and ride towards the safety of Medina. Ali's heart was as steady as a rock. He was calm. He was content. He was... happy.

If he died that night, it would be in the way of God. It would be a sacrifice to save the greatest man to walk this Earth. It would be a furtherance of God's mercy and grace to mankind through Muhammad.

As the Prophet slipped out of his home and into the night, Ali would recite the following verse of protection for his beloved cousin against his enemies:

And We have put a barrier before them and a barrier behind them, then We have blind-folded them, so they do not see. – Holy Quran, 36:9

Moments after the Prophet had escaped, Ali heard a faint noise outside the house. It was the sound of men whose hearts were filled with hate. The stench of evil pierced through the walls of the home. He heard them, he felt them, and he all but saw them in the darkness of the night. Footsteps came closer.

The gang of assassins were veiled. Nothing of them was visible, except for the glimmer of their unsheathed swords that were ready to spill blood on this quiet night. Swords drawn, they were now merely feet away from the bed of Muhammad.

Ali leaped to his feet, rising from beneath the sheets. The veiled assassins jumped back in shock. Ali drew his sword, one that shined brighter than the moon. Seeing the warrior towering above them, the assassins quivered in their boots.

"Ali?! We have come for Muhammad, where is he?!"

"You must come through me first."

One of the assassins, Khalid, would look to the ground and shake his head in disappointment. He sheathed his sword and walked out of the house, defeated. Ali remained in battle stance, sword in hand, until they were all gone. They did not dare to challenge Ali, for they knew it would lead to their demise. The depraved assassins were defeated, and the Prophet was saved.

That is how the days would unfold. When the Prophet was in danger, he made one call. That was to Ali, and Ali came through and through every single time. So much so that it would be said that, given all the attacks and onslaughts on the faith from its early days, "Islam would not have survived, except by the sword of Ali."

CHAPTER 6

THE TASTE OF DEFEAT

Take this sword, for your husband honored it. God annihilated the pagans of Quraysh by Ali's hand.

– Muhammad

Islam and its Prophet would come under attack on more than one occasion. It was not just the pagans of Mecca that wanted to assassinate Muhammad and be rid of this new prophet who called people to the oneness of God and the brotherhood of man. There were enemies all around. And as the scores of Arabs, Persians, and Africans coming into Islam grew, their enemies were watching closely. They were threatened by this growing faith and freedom that inspired so many people.

The idea that an Arab and a non-Arab were the same in the eyes of the One Lord was unheard of. The shade of your skin did not matter in the eyes of God, whether you were born into bondage or royalty – all the servants of God were free. It was a faith for all, but it resonated most with the disenfranchised. Youth, women, and all minorities alike were recognized, respected, and empowered. Those who benefitted from the status quo did not like that. So, Muhammad and his followers would face a series of battles, and there, defending the faith and the faithful, was Ali.

"There is no youth but Ali, and there is no sword but Dhulfiqar," was a statement in honor of Ali that the Prophet Muhammad had repeated on numerous occasions.

Ali's sword, Dhulfiqar, knew no match. It was a gift to him from the Holy Prophet, one that was sent down from the heavens by the Archangel Gabriel as a gift from God to Ali. Through this gift, the Muslims would be protected, and the honor of Islam would be preserved through justice.

At the Battle of Badr, Ali was a young man in his mid-twenties. The armies gathered at the open fields of Badr, a place that was in between the cities of Mecca and Medina. The Muslims were led by Hamza ibn Abd al-Muttalib, Ali ibn Abi Talib, and Ubayda ibn Alharith ibn Abd al-Muttalib, while Utba ibn Rubay'a commanded the Meccan army. The Muslim commanders would have their glory that day, and their glory was only for God. The same could not be said for the Meccans.

This was the first large-scale engagement between the Muslims and the Meccans, after several months of mini skirmishes. What started off as a defensive battle soon became an outstanding victory for the Muslims, who defeated the Meccans far before the sun would set that day. Several key nobles of Quraysh were killed, including one of the Prophet's earliest antagonists from the pagans of Mecca – Abu Jahal. The Muslims were victorious.

On that day, Ali single-handedly killed twenty-two Meccans, while the entire Muslim army killed twenty-seven. Although Ali's hand delivered a soothing touch to the orphans in the streets, he was a warrior who delivered justice against falsehood in the battlefield. He quickly established himself as the best warrior amongst the Muslims, and indeed in of all Arabia. Muhammad relied on him to strike such a victory for the Muslims, as no one could but Ali.

The Prophet would stand proud on that day, proclaiming the glory of God, as those fighting on the battlefield were not only the warriors of Islam, but also the heavenly angels led by the command of Archangel Gabriel. The strategic genius and the divine guidance of Muhammad ushered the Muslims into their grand victory.

"O' people of Qulayb... O' Utba ibn Rubay'a, Sheyba ibn Rubay'a, Umayya ibn Khalaf, and Abu Jahal ibn Hisham... Have you found what your lord promised to be true? Because I found what my lord promised me to be true!"

Those were the words of Prophet Muhammad at the conclusion of the battle. The Muslims cheered in celebration, prostrated in worship, and looked upon their champion in awe. Their prophet was Muhammad, and their champion was indeed Ali, the defender of the oppressed, the marginalized, and the Truth.

When the Meccan army returned home in defeat, their people did not receive it well. They were outraged. Anger filled the city and vengeance was in the air.

"Vengeance! Vengeance! Kill them! Kill them! Battle! Battle! We will not have Badr repeated, and the memory of that day shall be erased!" the Meccans rallied and shouted in the streets of their city.

It was a fury unlike any other they had seen in their recent history. They were determined to prepare a force to be reckoned with. "The Muslims will regret their victory," the pagans of Quraysh promised.

Abu Sufyan, now the de facto chieftain of Quraysh – the leading tribe in Mecca, was full of spite. He addressed the Meccans with a definitive speech. Abu Sufyan spoke to his people:

> O' people of Quraysh! Do not cry over your dead. Do not wail over them, and do not recite their elegies. Instead, be tough and resolute. If you are to cry and mourn over them, you will surely lose your anger. You will become complacent with what has happened and distance yourself from enmity you have for Muhammad and his companions. If they hear that you are mourning, they will gloat at you, and that would be the worse of the two tragedies we face. You must know the vengeance that is yours. From this moment, we will not sleep with our women nor will we eat meat until we kill Muhammad!

Abu Sufyan had this animosity for the several months that spanned between the Battle of Badr and what would be the Battle of Uhud. The Meccans mobilized their forces outside of Medina. The Muslims anticipated their attack and decided to meet them outside of the city, instead of waiting for the attack on their homes. Near the Mountain of Uhud, the two armies met once again.

The Meccan army of 3,000 was led by Abu Sufyan, Khalid ibn Al-Waleed, and Amr ibn Al-Aas. Talha ibn Abi Talha was the flagbearer of their forces. The Muslim army of 700 warriors had Mus'ab ibn 'Umayr as their flagbearer, with Hamza standing right behind him and Ali as their commander.

The Meccan objective in this battle was to rid themselves of Muhammad. They had three times the manpower and wanted to ensure that Muhammad would finally be killed. Though the Muslims endured a heavy blow to their forces, the Meccans were not successful in their objective.

The battle began with the Muslims, led by Ali, gaining considerable ground and blowing through the ranks of the Meccans, one after another. It had seemed as if victory was imminent for the smaller Muslim army. Their forces were strategically placed and they fought from higher grounds. Their archers in the rear flank thwarted the attacks of the Meccan cavalry that tried to take the Muslims by surprise. As the battle ensued and the plunder of war became apparent, those in the rear flank of the Muslim army abandoned their posts in order to capture the loot.

That maneuver weakened the Muslims' position and allowed for an onslaught on their ranks by the Meccans. Though the Prophet had specifically instructed them to resist the urge of abandoning their positions, the majority of the archers in the rear flank simply did not heed his call. For that, his life was put in danger.

At one point, only a few companions surrounded the Prophet while trying to fend off the Meccans. The Meccan cavalry attack was led by Khalid ibn Al-Waleed, who had broken through the ranks to get to Muhammad. The Prophet drew his own sword and engaged in combat to defend himself. They were that close.

As Ali was engaged in battle himself, striking through the rows of enemies in his midst, he knew the Prophet was in danger. Fighting through their defenses, he wished only to come to the aid of his prophet. The heat of battle had reached a point where the Prophet called out to him, "O' Ali, relieve me of this battalion…"

Hearing the Prophet's call, Ali would blaze through the enemy lines, slaying dozens, peeling the enemies off the small circle of the Prophet and his companions. Ali single-handled thwarted the attacks of Khalid ibn Al-Waleed and his fleet.

The battle went on until sunset. It exhausted both armies, devastating their ranks. Their swords were bent, and too many of their men slain. The Muslims lost Hamza ibn Abd al-Muttalib, "the Lion of God" as he was called, and Mus'ab, the flagbearer of the army. The Meccans, too, lost many of their own.

Abu Sufyan feared that they would lose too many more if they continued. Khalid ibn Al-Waleed gathered what remained of their forces and marched back to Mecca. Their hearts were filled with disappointment, anguish, and misery. Though they were able to take the lives of many Muslims that day, they did not kill Muhammad.

The Prophet returned with his army to Medina. Waiting for him was his beloved daughter, Fatima. She greeted her father, Muhammad, and husband, Ali, ready to relieve them of the weight of their armor. Ali was soaked in blood after thwarting so many of the enemies' attacks. As they entered, Ali handed her his sword, Dhulfiqar.

As Fatima took the sword with her two hands, the Prophet said to her, "Take this sword, for your husband honored it. God annihilated the pagans of Quraysh by Ali's hand." Fatima welcomed the heroes of battle with her warm embrace and loving smile.

Meanwhile, the pagans of Mecca were burning inside out. Muhammad could not be defeated! His religion continued to expand and the Muslims would flourish. His light could not be stopped, it would fill the Earth's darkness. It was like the light of day: as a new day would be born and the sun would rise, the light would only shine brighter from the heavenly sky.

Nevertheless, the Meccans hope would be reignited with a new ally. The Jews of Medina wanted to launch a war against the Muslims and thought to involve the Meccans to create a more formidable force against Muhammad's army. The Meccans quickly agreed, seeing they had another chance to take their vengeance against Muhammad and his followers. They would go on to launch the Battle of Khandaq – the Trench.

CHAPTER 7

THE BATTLE OF THE TRENCH

The duel between Ali and Amr on the Day of the Trench is greater in virtue than all of the deeds of my nation until the Day of Judgment.

– Muhammad

The Battle of the Trench was in the fifth year after *Hijra*, 627 AD. The Hijra refers to the Prophet's migration from Mecca to Medina – a declaration of a new age and the rise of the Muslim community after Meccan persecution. It was that year that some groups within the Jewish community in Medina mobilized their forces against the Muslims. These groups, like the pagans of Mecca, were threatened by the rise of the new religion and its followers.

Leaders from the Jewish community went to the chiefs of Quraysh, namely Abu Sufyan, inviting them to join in yet another attack on Muhammad and his followers. Quraysh was elated to receive such an invitation. Abu Sufyan gathered his people and mobilized another army to join in attacking the Muslims again. There were over 10,000 soldiers that marched on to Medina, led by Abu Sufyan.

When the Prophet was informed of their advancement, a group of his followers quickly gathered around him to discuss how to protect the city of Medina from such a force. A suggestion was made by one of the Prophet's companions, Salman "al-Farisi", the Persian. Salman was one of the most intelligent, faithful, and committed followers of Muhammad.

Medina was protected from three of its sides, due to its natural mountainous landscape and surrounding groundwater levels. One side, however, was vulnerable to attack. Salman recommended that they dig a great trench on that vulnerable side to protect the city from invasion. With such a trench, the enemy would find it nearly impossible to reach the city and its inhabitants. He spoke of the tactic from experience in military combat and strategy that he had garnered in his homeland. The group thought it as a great idea and supported Salman's suggestion.

The Prophet approved and within moments, the Muslims went to work. Every single able-bodied Muslim helped dig this great trench, including the Prophet himself. They say it took six days to complete. Afterwards, they mobilized a force of 3,000 warriors to face the thousands that came from Mecca.

When the Meccans arrived and found the massive trench, there was not much they could do. For several weeks they created a siege around Medina. The forces exchanged arrows and spears at a distance, but nothing more. Finally, a small group of Quraysh's best warriors decided enough was enough. Led by Amr ibn Abduwud, they were able to find a confined path to get beyond the trench and found themselves before the Muslims. The legends of the time spoke of the strength and ferocity of Amr. The Arabs said that he was stronger than a thousand men in battle.

Amr bellowed into the ranks of the Muslims, "Is there any man here to challenge me?!"

No one answered. Only silence.

He repeated his call, and again was met with silence.

The Muslims were terrified of Amr. They knew who he was, and therefore no one dared to accept his challenge. The Prophet would look at his companions and say, "Who amongst you will accept his challenge?"

Again, no one responded.

One of the youngest amongst them would wait no longer and answered to the Prophet's call.

"I will, O' Messenger of God!" Ali said firmly.

It was no surprise that Ali would rise to the occasion, but the Prophet wanted to see who other than Ali would seize the moment and answer the call. Who would be brave enough to face the most feared warrior in Arabia with a heart filled with faith in the One True God?

Hence, the Prophet asked Ali to retreat.

Again, Amr would repeat his challenge before the Muslims. Not a single man moved an inch or uttered a sound. Ali would stand again, waiting for the Prophet's permission to engage.

Muhammad looked at his cousin and walked towards him. He embraced Ali and kissed him on his forehead. The Prophet then took off his turban and dressed Ali with it. He said a prayer for Ali and sent him into the battlefield. Like the lion of the battlefield, Ali would rush to face off with Amr. He stood before him within moments.

Looking at the young Ali before him, Amr would smirk and chuckle. "Did Muhammad not find anyone younger than you to come fight me?" He asked sarcastically. "By God, I would not want to kill you and bring sorrow to your mother…"

"But by God, I would love to kill you…" Ali would smile back at Amr.

Amr's smirk was wiped off his face. He was overcome with rage. Who is this young man that would dare to speak to him in such a way?

Before their swords would meet, Ali being Ali, with every movement guided by justice, said to Amr, "I invite you to the path of God and faith in the message of His Prophet Muhammad…"

Amr would irritably reply, "I have no need for that! There is no choice but combat now."

"As you wish," Ali calmly replied.

Their swords clashed, and from all their swift motions in the sands of Medina, a cloud of dust formed around them. The spectators could no longer see them clearly. As both sides cheered, they quieted for a few moments, waiting for the dust to settle.

"Allahu Akbar!" God is great! The Muslims called out, as they saw Ali standing above the body of Amr. The Muslims cheered as the man who was equal to a thousand warriors lay at the feet of their champion, Ali. Just before Ali was about to take Amr's life with a final strike, Amr mustered the energy to spit in Ali's face.

In that moment, Ali lowered his sword and stepped back from the defeated Amr. He turned around and began walking.

Amr called out, "Where are you going, Ali? Come back and end my misery!"

Ali walked away for a few minutes. As Amr would continue to yell in agony, the Muslims were perplexed as to why Ali walked away. They continued to watch as Ali paced back and forth in those moments. Ali would finally return to Amr to give him the final strike and end his life. The man who stood equal to a thousand men was dead. The might of a thousand men could not withstand the valor of Ali.

The Muslims cheered and encircled their champion in celebration. One of the Muslim soldiers was still perplexed by Ali's actions and was adamant on asking him about it.

"O' Ali, why did you walk away from Amr before striking him? You turned away, walked for a few moments and returned... why?" he asked Ali.

Ali turned to him and said, "Amr spat in my face just before I was to deliver the final blow to send him to his death. In that moment, my strike could have been to avenge my own pride. It would have been a strike of anger and in the heat of passion, it may have no longer been for the One God..."

Mesmerized by his words, the companion would nod and listen on.

"I walked away to realign my focus to God and returned to finish him."

The Muslims were in awe of this spiritual titan warrior who was in their midst. Who would have the presence of heart and mind to act so decisively and so definitively? It was enough that he had the courage to challenge him, to overpower him, yet Ali went beyond this. He would also only strike his foe with an intention that was reserved for the Almighty, without an ounce of self-righteousness. That was Ali.

The enemies were furious. Defeated once again, the pagans of Mecca would continue to hold their grudge against the Muslims and their prophet. But their attack on Medina would not be left at the trenches. The Prophet decided to take the battle to them.

CHAPTER 8

KHAYBAR

The strength I exerted at Khaybar was for God, here I break the bread for myself...

– Ali

"I will give the flag tomorrow to a man that loves God and His Messenger, and God and His Messenger love him... He pursues his enemies and never flees from battle," the Prophet promised his companions this at Khaybar.

Khaybar was a Jewish oasis town, north of Medina, notorious for the monumental fortress that protected its city. It was an extension of the community of Jews who had waged war on the Prophet. Though some in the Jewish community respected Islam and the Muslims, the men at Khaybar were hostile to the new faith and its prophet.

The Prophet would mobilize his forces and make their way to the impenetrable fort town. At their arrival, Muhammad would raise his blessed hands to the sky and offer the following prayer to God,

"O' Lord of the Heavens... O' Lord of the Earths... O' Lord of the winds... we ask you the best of what is in this village, and the best of its people, and we beseech you from the evil within it and its people…"

He lowered his hands back to his sides and turned around to face his men.

"Carry on in the name of God," he ordered them to attack Khaybar.

The first battalion of the Muslim army to attack was led by Abu Bakr. They were unable to break through the gates of Khaybar. On the second day, Umar ibn Al-Khattab led a battalion to achieve what his comrade Abu Bakr could not on the first day of their arrival. He was also unsuccessful. The Prophet was not disappointed. He did not lash out at his men, nor did he demean them for their failed efforts. Instead, he smiled and touched their shoulders.

"Tomorrow, I will give the flag to man who loves God and His Messenger, and God and His Messenger love him… God will open this path by his hands, and he will not flee," the Prophet told his companions.

Umar would later say, "I did not wish for any position at all, except on that day… as I hoped to be the one who God and His Messenger love…" Like Umar, the rest of the Muslims continued to wonder, who would this man be that God and His Messenger love? Who is this man that does not flee, and through whom, God will open the impenetrable gates of Khaybar? Why was it still a question? Was it not obvious that there was only one man to answer the Prophet's call? Still, they waited.

The night seemed long and ever so dark, as the Muslims waited anxiously for the man who would bring them divine victory. When the morning finally came, they joined their ranks and held onto their swords and spears. Their hearts pounded in their chests, their eyes scanned the horizons, and their ears stayed to the ground. Listening. Watching. Waiting.

The Prophet's voice would pierce through the silence, "Where is Ali?" he asked.

Ali had removed himself from the battlefield. His eyes had become infected and therefore he could not see. Nonetheless, he heard the Prophet's call and so he answered. He walked toward the Prophet and offered his service. Muhammad would soon see that Ali was in no condition to fight. As his cousin stood before him, Muhammad saw the pain and severe inflammation of Ali's eyes.

The Prophet took a step closer towards his cousin, and slowly placed his hands over Ali's eyes. After a moment, Muhammad removed his hands and watched as Ali opened his eyes. He gazed upon the glorious face of Muhammad, with eyes healed by his blessed touch.

"Give me the flag," the Prophet ordered his soldiers.

They brought the flag to the Prophet, and he raised it up high. He waved the flag in three motions and then handed it to Ali.

"Take this flag, and carry on until God opens your path," he said to Ali.

What would only be a few minutes felt like an eternity as the Muslims watched in anticipation. Ali walked toward the gates of Khaybar. Before reaching its enormous gates, Ali was met by their champion – the most feared warrior of the Jews – Marhab.

Marhab announced his presence and made it clear to all those watching who he was.

"I am Marhab. Khaybar knows who I am. I am the tested warrior, thrusting with my spear and striking with my sword when lions advance in the raging flames of war!"

To that, Ali replied, "I am the one whose mother named him Haidar – the Lion. Like a lion, I strike fear in the hearts of the enemies and return their attacks with one that is fiercer than they have ever seen."

Within moments, the warriors engaged in combat. Only after the second blow, Ali managed to strike Marhab on the helmet, splitting his skull in half. Marhab was immediately killed. Ali proceeded to the gate. They say that Ali had lost the shield and had no tools to lift or pry open the gate of the fortress. Prior to Ali, over a dozen of the men had tried to pry open the gate, but were unsuccessful. Ali stood before the gate, and with his two bare hands, lifted the doors of the gate, prying it out from its hinges. Ali first held the gate with one hand as a shield from the enemies, and then jumped into the moat and made a bridge, using the pried door for the Muslims to make their way into the fortress.

The Muslims saw victory at the hands of Ali. The hands that God used to open their path, as the Prophet promised. The most beautiful thing about this young Ali was his grace. Though he was the most valiant and fierce warrior, he fought selflessly and sought no fame. He monitored his intentions with every step on the way to battle. With every stroke of his sword, and every swing of his spear, he whispered the praises of God. And when he struck his enemies, he glorified His most High name.

After the battle, the Muslims would gather to eat and rest. Between the two or three different options of food, Ali made his choice – dry bread. That was a normal go-to for Ali. That, or a handful of dates, or perhaps a cup of yogurt. His diet was simple, and his portions were small.

"One third for water, one third for food, and one third to breathe…" Ali used to say.

Ali took a piece of bread that was a bit larger than he wanted, so he decided to piece it in half. The bread was dry and hard and was not breaking between Ali's two palms. So, Ali took the loaf of bread and broke it on his knee. The companions in his midst looked at him in disbelief.

"O' Ali, you just single-handedly yanked out the gate of Khaybar, a feat that dozens of men could not do together, but now, in this instance, we see you breaking a loaf of bread on your knee?" a companion inquired, perplexed.

Ali smiled.

"The strength I exerted at Khaybar was for God; here I break the bread for myself," he replied simply.

CHAPTER 9

THE CONQUEST OF MECCA

Rather, it is that of the Message…

– Abbas ibn Abd al-Muttalib

In the eigth year after Hijra, 630AD, the Prophet would make it his mission to free Mecca from the hold of Quraysh. In every attack and every battle, the pagans of Quraysh were defeated. Their morale was low, and they became fewer in number. Throughout this period, Meccans defected from Quraysh and moved to Medina to convert to Islam and pledge allegiance to Muhammad. The light of Islam was spreading across Arabia, and it was only a matter of time before the House of God would be liberated from the idols of Quraysh.

The hour of conquest had come. It was the holy month of Ramadan and the Prophet mobilized a force of 10,000 soldiers to march on to Mecca. The Prophet and the greatest force he had assembled yet stood at the outskirts of Mecca. The flag of the Muslims was handed to Saad ibn Ubada, the leader of the Ansar, the people that welcomed the Prophet into Medina.

Saad waved the flag zealously. All eyes were on Saad. "Onward!" Valiantly riding on his horse, Saad made his way to the city of Mecca. With every gallop, Saad grew in fervor. He remembered the persecution the Prophet faced at the hands of the Meccans. He remembered the Muslims who were tortured and killed by the pagans of Quraysh. He remembered the scores of families that migrated to his city, escaping persecution and humiliation. With all the images in his mind, he was filled with rage.

As he arrived at the gates of Mecca, Saad's eyes looked crazed with spite.

"Today is the day of massacre! Today your families will be taken captive!" Saad would yell out.

But that was not the call of Muhammad. That was not within the ordained sanctions of Islam. Muhammad had come forth with the religion of peace and harmony, not of war and vengeance. Though Saad was good a man, and a loyal companion of the Prophet, he was overcome by a furious passion. Such passion, if not tamed, could turn to transgression.

Hearing Saad's war cry, the Prophet feared the tragedy that would befall Mecca. Even with all the pain of persecution and oppression he experienced, Muhammad wished no harm upon the Meccans. In the end, he was sent as a mercy to all, and his return to Mecca was to complete God's favor upon his people.

The Prophet turned to those in his ranks to see who could quickly replace Saad before the fire in his heart torched the lands of Mecca. Who was a fearless champion in battle, yet the most pious in his prayer? Who drew his sword at the call of justice, but calculated every strike in the name of God alone? Who gave his life with thanks and prostrated for the glory of God time and time again? Muhammad could see only one man in his ranks with such virtues.

"O' Ali, go forth and aid Saad... take the flag from him, and be the one who enters Mecca with it," said the Prophet. Seeing Ali, Saad would comply and hand over the flag to him as the Prophet ordered.

Ali entered Mecca with valor and chivalry witnessed by few. For any other commander, today would have been his day. A day of vengeance and victory over the enemy. A day to deliver justice for all the pain they had caused him, his family, and his brethren. Ali saw the treachery of the Meccans from day one as a young man.

His life was threatened on too many occasions. But Ali was different. He held no grudges in his heart. He had no desire for vengeance. He drew his sword only for God. For when his faith was attacked, he was that warrior who stood staring death in the eyes, reacting only with a smile.

It was with that smile that he entered Mecca. The smile of faith and certainty, one that he learned from his prophet, Muhammad. As Ali rode into Mecca, he had such a calming feel to him. People watched him in awe. Moments ago, they were terrified by the war cries of Saad, and now they saw the young Ali riding with a smile. It was as if his conquest was an invitation of peace, not of war. That is what Ali did so beautifully. Though he was unmatched on the battlefield, his battle was not void of humanity. He did not thirst for blood, he yearned for justice. He was not rejoiced with fallen enemies; he desired peace and the protection of the innocent.

The nobles of Quraysh, led by Abu Sufyan, would lay down their swords before a battle would ensue. They saw the grandeur of the Prophet's forces, led by Ali, and chose forfeit over bloody defeat. As the Muslim army marched into Mecca without spilling blood, Abu Sufyan would look on with rancor in his heart. At one point, he stood next to the Prophet's uncle, Abbas ibn Abd al-Muttalib, and shared a thought:

"It seems like your nephew's possessions and dominion have expanded greatly..."

Abbas took pause as he gazed at the ranks of Islam's thousands of warriors.

"Rather, it is that of the Message," Abbas replied as he continued to look proudly at the marching men of Islam.

Mecca was liberated. The Muslims were able to circumambulate the Kaaba and perform their holy pilgrimage once again, without fear of persecution. The tribes were united under the banner of God and his Prophet. But what would happen when God's Prophet was no more?

CHAPTER 10

GHADEER KHUM

Congratulations, O' son of Abu Talib, with the rise and fall of the sun,
you are my master, and the master of every believing man and woman!

– Umar ibn Al-Khattab

In the tenth year after Hijra, 632AD, the Muslims were informed that the Prophet would perform the pilgrimage, and that this one could very well be his last.

The message was spread by ambassadors of the Prophet to the entire nation, to join the Prophet in what would become known as his "Farewell Pilgrimage". Tens of thousands would come to Mecca for this pilgrimage, to enjoy the honor of being led by the Holy Prophet in the rituals of Hajj.

Whenever the Holy Prophet had an expedition or journey outside of the city, he would leave a viceroy behind in the city for all administrative matters. When he was nearing leaving the abode of this world, it was no different.

When the Prophet completed the rituals of Hajj and was on his way back home, he was given a divine order to stop his caravan. The Archangel Gabriel descended from the Heavens and relayed the verse to God's most beloved prophet:

O' Messenger, proclaim what has been revealed to you from
your Lord; and if you do not, then you have not delivered
His message, and God will protect you from the people;
surely God will not guide the unbelieving people. – Holy
Quran 5:67

What proclamation was so significant to stop a caravan of
thousands of Muslims in the middle of the desert after an ex-
hausting pilgrimage?

They had reached a place called Ghadeer Khum. The time of
prayer was near. The Prophet commanded his people to gather
those who had gone ahead, along with those who had trailed behind, to come together at Ghadeer Khum. Prayers were to be led
by the people's prophet.

Before they were to shake each other's hands and exchange
their brotherly smiles at the conclusion, the Prophet wished to
speak to his people. The sun scorched the Arabian desert sands,
and the Muslims laid out any extra layers of clothing they had to
relieve their burning feet. Before prayer, a pulpit was assembled
by the companions, made of boulders and saddles.

The Prophet desired, by divine will, to address his people at
such a historical point in the last year of his life. It was as if the
combination of stone and leather was a symbolic combination
of permanence for the statements the Prophet was about to
make.

Muhammad called upon Ali. They ascended the makeshift
pulpit and peered across the thousands of Muslims awaiting the

words of their prophet. Ali stood to the right side of his brother, as he did throughout the entirety of his life.

> O' people, I am being called back to my Lord, and there is no doubt that I will answer the call. I am leaving amongst you two weighty things, if you hold on to these two things, you will never stray after me: The Book of God, and my progeny - the people of my household. These two will not separate until they are returned to me at the Pool in the Hereafter.

A pin drop could be heard in the desert's silence, though it was filled by thousands of its natives. The various colors of Arabian dress covered the sands as the Muslims sat and listened to their wise leader. Muhammad spoke and they listened. He inspired their hearts and invigorated their souls.

As he looked upon the masses of his followers, he asked them a consequential question.

"O' people, do I not have more mastership over you than you do over yourselves?" Muhammad asked his followers.

"Yes O' Messenger of God!" they replied in unison.

He repeated the question and the people answered again in the same. The Prophet then took Ali by the hand and raised Ali's hand high for all to see.

"For whoever I am his master, this Ali is his master! May God support those who support him, be an enemy to those who oppose him, help those who help him, and let down those that let him down... and may the Truth turn with him wherever he may turn."

The call of prayer came, and the Prophet led his people in prayer. At the conclusion of prayer, the Prophet ordered his followers to pay their allegiance to Ali as the nation's leader after him. A small tent was set up under which Ali and Muhammad stood. One after the other, thousands of Muslims came to Ali and placed their hand in his hand, paying homage to the successor of Islam's Prophet.

The Prophet stood by with a bright smile. Indeed, this was a joyous day for him. He had a successor. The people knew who he was and paid allegiance before him. The Prophet could leave the world knowing that the trust of God was being delivered and guidance was proclaimed.

Among those who entered the tent to give allegiance was Umar ibn Al-Khattab. As he placed his hand in the rugged hand of Ali, he said, "Congratulations, O' son of Abu Talib, with the rise and fall of the sun, you are my master, and the master of every believing man and woman…"

It was a glorious day of celebration. To make his mark on the day, the notable Arabian poet, Hassan ibn Thabit, asked the Prophet if he could recite a few verses in honor of the event. The Prophet smiled and nodded in consent.

> Beside the Ghadeer (pond) of the valley of Khum
> the Prophet calls upon those close and afar
> so hear carefully wherever you are!
> He inquired, 'Who is your Master and Wali?'
> with sincerity and zest the crowd roared,
> 'Our Master is our Lord, while you are our Wali,

You shall find today none willing to disobey.'
He then called upon Ali and spoke with his heart,
'Stand up, O Ali, there is only you as guide after I depart.'

Muhammad declared, "Ali is from me and I am from Ali, and he is the master of every believer after me." Though this may have been the most magnanimous proclamation of Ali's leadership and succession to the Prophet, especially with such close proximity to the end of Muhammad's life, the Prophet announced Ali's status on numerous occasions during his lifetime.

Upon the migration of the Muslims to the city of Medina, the Prophet gathered the Muhajiroun and Ansar, those who migrated from Mecca and the natives of Medina, respectively. He created a pact of brotherhood between the two groups. In fact, he personally matched each Muhajir with a brother from the Ansar. All of the Muhajiroun and all of the Ansar were given brothers, except for one Muslim – Ali.

Ali walked up to his cousin, with his eyes sadly cast down to the ground, and said, "O' Messenger of God, you have assigned everyone a brother except me. Who will be my brother?"

The Prophet smiled at Ali, embraced him and said, "O' Ali, there is no brother for you but me, for you are my brother, my heir, and my successor…"

In similar embraces the Prophet would profess to his brother, with others in their midst to witness, "You are to me as Aaron was to Moses, except that there is no prophet after me." It was clear that there would be no brother to the Prophet but Ali. For no one possessed the virtues and excellence of the Prophet quite like Ali.

Ali was the Prophet's champion warrior on the battlefield. He led the Muslims into glory in every battle. Never did Ali face an opponent and not reign as the champion of that confrontation. But the champion's triumphs were not only on the battlefield. He exemplified what it meant to be a true follower of Islam and its Prophet. Whether it be in the marketplace, the home, or the mosque, Ali was that heavenly prince of virtue who everyone could not help but love.

One day, as Ali prayed in the mosque of Medina, a feat of virtue took place that was recognized by the Holy Quran itself. A beggar, dressed in ragged clothes, was begging outside of the mosque that day, but had no luck with the Muslims of the town. Trying his chances, he decided to ask for help inside the mosque. So, the beggar entered the mosque and begged the mosque-goers as they came and left the house of God. As the beggar went from one person to the next, he was left disenchanted. Once again, no one would help him.

About to leave the mosque disappointed, he saw Ali immersed in his prayer. Ali was in mid-prayer in the position of *Rukoo*, bowing before his Lord. As the beggar looked closer, he noticed Ali's right hand was extended out towards him. The beggar walked up to Ali and soon was elated. In Ali's hand was his ring. His extended hand gestured to the beggar that it was his gift to the beggar. The beggar took the ring, praised God for Ali's generosity, and merrily went on his way. Ali continued his prayer and in those moments, the verse was revealed to the Prophet by the Angel Gabriel:

Your guardian is only Allah, His Apostle, and the faithful who maintain the prayer and give the zakat while bowing down. – Holy Quran 5:55

Muhammad would emphasize the virtues and excellence of Ali on a number of occasions throughout his lifetime. Ali was not only praised by the Prophet, but he was also compared to and described as the reflection of the prophets that came before him. Abuthar al-Ghafari tells of a time that the companions were gathered around the Prophet under the open sky. As they sat amongst each other, benefiting from the Prophet's guidance and wisdom on that beautiful day, Muhammad suddenly stood up, bowed, and then prostrated, giving thanks to God. He then turned to his companions with his prophetic smile and spoke:

Whoever wants to see Adam in his knowledge, Noah in his understanding, Abraham in his friendship, Moses in his intimate prayers, Jesus in his journeying, and Job in his patience during calamity, look at the man coming forth. He is like the sun and the moon in radiance, and like the stars shining so bright. His heart is the bravest of all people and his hand is most generous. May the curse of God, the angels, and the people be upon those who hate him.

The companions of the Prophet turned to see who the man coming towards them as the Prophet described. It was none other than Ali.

When the Prophet left Medina for the Battle of Tabuk, he appointed Ali as the leader of the city before embarking on his journey. "I cannot leave without having you as my viceroy," the Prophet would say to Ali before departing. He continued with saying, "Every prophet has a guardian and heir, and my guardian and heir is Ali ibn Abi Talib."

The matter of leadership over the Muslims was not left without decree. The Prophet would not leave his nation orphaned. He would not, he could not. Ali was the chosen Imam – the leader. He would be the Prophet's Caliph – successor. He was indeed the Prophet's heir.

And to make it clear where loyalty and hostility lay in the matter of belief, the Prophet instructed his followers with a clear statement: "Whoever fights the Imam of their time will die as a disbeliever." This would be remembered in battles to come.

The Prophet told his people and made it clear, "Ali and I are the fathers of this nation." As fathers of the nation, the Prophet established that he was "the Master of Prophets and Ali is the Master of Guardians." In fact, he made it clear who all his successors were through his declaration, "The guardians after me are twelve. The first of them is Ali ibn Abi Talib and the last of them is the Mahdi."

In honoring the decree of God to follow His appointed Prophet and Imams, the lovers of light continue to journey down this path of life. They journey with a moral compass in hand, bettering their lives, and the lives of all of those around them. This moral compass was established by and through the love of

Muhammad and Ali, for Muhammad guided his admirers through the door of Ali. On numerous occasions, he reminded his companions and followers with this truth:

> My Lord commanded me to close all the doors except the door of Ali.

> Ali is the door of my knowledge, and the one who will clarify for my nation that which I was sent with.

> Love for Ali is faith, and hatred for Ali is hypocrisy.

> Ali is the partition between Heaven and Hell.

> The title of the believer's book is love for Ali.

> Ali is the door of servitude, and whoever passes through that door is a true believer.

> I am the City of Knowledge and Ali is its Gate.

The Prophet's emphasis on the love for and adherence to Ali was a recurring theme in his guidance. The family of Ali were part and parcel of Muhammad's message, both in word and conduct. The Prophet was rarely seen without Ali or his sons, Hasan and Husayn. The young boys would accompany their grandfather, Muhammad, as he prayed in the mosque and gave sermons to his companions. The boys, being no more than five and six years old, were often found sitting on the Prophet's lap as he spoke to his followers. He would play with them and make them giggle. So full of joy, he would point to his grandsons and say, "Hasan and Husayn are the Princes of the Youth of Paradise."

When the Prophet was asked by his followers in Medina how they could best serve him and repay him for guiding them to the light, his reply would be simple yet profound:

I do not ask you any reward for it except the love of [my] near of kin.

When asked, "Who is your near of kin O' Messenger of God?" He said, "They are Ali, Fatima, Hasan, and Husayn." The love of his family is all he asked.

CHAPTER 11

RETURN OF THE BELOVED

Then take that ease gifted by my Lord and give it to my people. Instead, give me their pain.

– Muhammad

The tenth year after Hijra would come to a close. The Prophet warned his people of his final days. Though they were experiencing a glory they had never seen before, everything would have an end. "And every soul shall taste death," he told his followers – even Muhammad.

In his last days, the Prophet was especially concerned with the state of his people. His nation was still young, and people could easily be disunited and misguided. The announcement of Ghadeer Khum weeks earlier made it clear to the Muslims, on such a large scale, where guidance would be derived after the Prophet's passing. The Prophet emphasized the importance of his family as the counterpart to the Word of God. He would raise the hand of Ali for all to see, as his caliph, his successor, his heir.

It was not merely a declaration of political successorship, or simply a proclamation of love and endearment: it was all, and everything. The Prophet did not speak out of whim. Every step he took and every word he uttered was inspired by revelation. Still, it was as if this was not enough.

On his deathbed, the Prophet looked around to see the many who had gathered in his home during his last days. They busied themselves in their circles of conversation, some talking about small things, and others about grand ideas for the future.

"Bring me a pen and scroll, so I shall write for you something from which you will never stray after me," the Prophet cut through the chatter.

They looked at one another and paused. Between the contradicting eyes of hope and the grimaces in the gathering, they asked themselves… what is the Prophet trying to do right now?

"He wants to make sure you all know who will take his place when he dies!" Some exclaimed.

Others replied, "The Prophet is overcome by pain. You have the Quran. God's book is enough for you…"

The exchange continued and it only grew louder. The room was filled with men arguing back and forth on the Prophet's request, as he lay there beside them. Then, one of the companions would yell out and silence them all, "He is hallucinating!"

Those words pierced the ears of the company, and those gathered, but more importantly the heart of the Prophet. The fact of the matter was that those who wanted to bring the Prophet what he requested were simply not strong enough before the disruption and audacity of those who said he had gone mad. They had raised their voices above the voice of their

Prophet and accused him of losing his mind. So, the Prophet would end the dispute amongst his competing followers and say, "After what you have just said, get up and leave now..."

The sad truth was that some of his followers stopped following his directives as soon as they learned of his illness. Just one day after he had fallen ill, the Prophet ordered for a force to be mobilized and sent to Damascus to battle the killers of one of his companions and military commanders, Zayd ibn Haritha. The battalion to fight in the name of the fallen companion, Zayd, was led by the martyr's son, Usama ibn Zayd. The Prophet intentionally ordered all of the personalities of the Muhajiroun, and the Ansar, to follow Usama in this conquest. These included companions like Abu Bakr, Umar ibn Al-Khattab, Abu Ubayda ibn Al-Jarrah, Saad ibn Abi Waqqas, and Saeed ibn Zayd, amongst others.

They did not mobilize, and they were slow to support Usama ibn Zayd in his campaign to Damascus. Upon hearing that the forces did not leave, and the companions did not join the ranks of Usama, the Prophet left his home and ascended the pulpit. His voice filled with fury and passion; he called out to his people:

What is this I hear that some of you have disobeyed my appointment of Usama as a commander over you? In this, you have disobeyed my appointment of his father before him as well! I swear that he was befitting of command, and his son after him is befitting of such command. He was one of the most beloved people to me... Be good to him, for he is of the virtuous amongst you.

Days later, the Prophet's condition would only worsen. His body grew weak and he would come to and from consciousness.

At one point, he woke up and asked of the status of Usama's campaign. He was told that Usama had yet to make his journey because the majority of the chief companions did not answer his call. Usama remained on the outskirts of Medina, waiting for the people to support his ranks, but to no avail.

The Prophet was again deeply hurt. He did not hide his anger from the many in his midst. He said, "Support the convoy of Usama, may God damn those who desert him."

The Prophet expressed a deliberate emphasis on following the convoy of Usama. History would tell that he wanted to clear the way for Ali's leadership after his demise. While he requested that Ali stay behind in Medina to administer the affairs of the state as his heir-apparent, there were a number of individuals within his community that he saw as an opposition to Ali's authority. The Prophet ordered them along with the rest of the people to join the ranks of Usama. But they refused.

The Prophet saw that his proclamations of Ali's caliphate and leadership were not enough to realize Ali's control over the state. The people's mutiny was clear, even before the Prophet passed, with their dissonance in following Usama's convoy. The reality broke the heart of Muhammad, as he foresaw the many troubles that his nation would face as they began to stray even before his eyes would forever close in this lowly abode.

The final day came. On his death bed, he came in and out of consciousness a few times. At one point, he opened his eyes and said, "Bring me my brother and companion."

His wife, Aisha, said, "Bring him Abu Bakr!" while Hafsa called out, "Bring him Umar!"

Hearing this, the Prophet repeated and exclaimed, "Bring me my brother and companion!"

Moving past Aisha and Hafsa, Um Salama said, "Bring him Ali, for he does not want anyone but him."

Ali came forth and sat at his brother's bedside. The Prophet's eyes lit up as his beloved came close. They embraced one another for so long that it was as if that embrace lasted for eternity. But even eternity was too short. The Prophet whispered to Ali for a while, until he fell asleep in Ali's arms. After some moments, Ali would leave Muhammad to rest.

As he left the room, people gathered around him and asked with eyes wide open, "What was it that the Prophet whispered to you Ali?"

"He advised me with what I am prepared to do, God willing."

The final hour of the Prophet came. Ali was at his side. Muhammad turned to his brother slowly and said, as his eyes lit up:

"O' Ali, place my head in your lap for the call of God has come. Direct my face toward the Qibla. Take care of my affairs and be the first to pray over my body. Do not leave me until you have placed me in my grave. And beseech God, the Most High…"

With a heavy heart, Ali obliged. He placed his brother's head in his lap and within moments the soul of God's Prophet began to depart. As the Angel of Death reluctantly began reaping his blessed soul, the Prophet felt the undeniable pangs of death.

Muhammad said, "O' Ezrael, is death truly this painful for all?"

The mighty angel lowered his wings and bashfully replied, "O' Beloved, God ordered me to make your death the least painful out of His love and adoration for you…"

"Then take that ease gifted by my Lord and give it to my people. Instead, give me their pain."

The skies turned dark and the people stood in disbelief. Could it be that the Mercy to Mankind was taken back to the Heavens? What a tragedy that words could not describe, nor could any form of expression fulfill the agony felt by a lover of Muhammad. Still the divine reality tells us…

Muhammad is but an apostle; [other] apostles have passed before him. If he dies or is slain, will you turn back on your heels? – Holy Quran 3:144

The Beloved Muhammad returned to his Lord. Ascended to the heavens once again. Still, the hearts of his nearest of kin ached like they had never before. And what was to come were dark days and even darker nights for the loving family of Muhammad.

CHAPTER 12

SAQEEFA & THE NEW CALIPHATE

You are not safe until you pay allegiance...

– Umar ibn Al-Khattab

As the news of the Prophet's death spread, it continued to shock people. Ali ibn Abi Talib, by orders of the Prophet, led the burial rituals. Alongside him were a number of relatives from Banu Hashim, as well as some companions from both the Muhajiroun and Ansar.

When hearing the news, not all were impressed to join in the burial rituals. Instead, a group of Ansar decided to meet at the *Saqeefa* of Banu Saaida to deliberate on the matter of the caliphate. The "Saqeefa" was a covered patio or gathering place, in which the Saaida clan gathered and met frequently. In this meeting, they were going to decide who amongst them would be the leader of the Muslims. They were close to paying allegiance to their own, Saad ibn Ubada as the Caliph, but some of the Muhajiroun got wind of the meeting, as they themselves were meeting to discuss the very same thing.

Abu Bakr, Umar ibn Al-Khattab, and Abu Ubayda ibn Jarrah interrupted the meeting at Saqeefa. The room quickly turned into a faceoff between two groups – the Muhajiroun against the Ansar. Uninvited to this private meeting, the Muhajiroun were a clear threat to the Ansar and vice versa. The tension grew as the opposing parties stared each other down, knowing that they stood in the way of each other's ambition to hold the caliphate.

Being a noble of the Muhajiroun, Umar stepped forward encircled by the attendees of Saqeefa and threatened the Ansar:

> The Arabians will not accept you as leaders over them, when their prophet has not come from you. They will not be opposed to a caliph that comes from the same place their prophet came, and that their leader is from amongst them. And we have that, over anyone who may contest from amongst the Arabs, as a clear argument and an apparent authority. And whoever fights us in the sultanate and emirate of Muhammad, as we are his successors and tribesmen, will be calling for falsehood, engaging in sin, or bringing upon himself his own destruction...

The threat was not received well by the Ansar. Still, a speaker amongst them would stand and reply to Umar's declaration with the following speech:

> O' Ansar! Take hold of this matter and do not heed to the words of this man and his friends. They will take from you what is yours. If they refuse to follow you in what you assume, then kick them out of these lands and take authority over them. By God, you are of a greater right in this over them, for it is by your swords that this religion has thrived...

But by God, if you wish, we will take it all back through mutilation! By God, with my sword I will pummel the snout of any man who stands against what I say!

Why were the Ansar and Muhajiroun arguing over who had greater right over the caliphate when the matter had already been decided by their prophet just weeks prior? Why was this such a point of contention? Why was it even a matter to be discussed? Was it not the very same companions who came forward at Ghadeer Khum, congratulated Ali, and pledged to Muhammad to follow his brother just days ago? As the tribes shouted back and forth with further threats of violence and aggression, where was the one that they had already paid allegiance to in the presence of the Prophet? Where was the Prophet's heir? Where was Ali?

Ali, along with other close companions of the Prophet, were busy with the burial rituals for the late Prophet. It had only been a few of hours since his soul had departed. Ali and his companions were not apprised of Saqeefa, or any other meeting in that regard.

Though the meeting at Saqeefa spoke about affiliation and closeness to the Prophet and his tribe, none of the Banu Hashim were present. The meeting did not have any representatives from the Prophet's family. Perhaps that is why there was so much in ruckus and bickering. In a move to bring the meeting to order, Umar nominated Abu Bakr for the position of Caliph and called the conveners to join him in pledging allegiance to him. In short, the hastiness of Saqeefa elected a new leader, and before the sun had set on that day, Abu Bakr was named as the Caliph of the Muslims.

Those who were present in the ordeal of Saqeefa did not attend the Prophet's burial, as the two events took place at the same time. This meeting apparently took priority over mourning the Prophet. Abu Bakr, Umar, and Abu Ubayda agreed that allegiance had to be given to the new caliphate across Muslim society to bring unity and order for the young community. The people were apprised of this quickly and knew that it would be taken by force if needed. They went to the Prophet's mosque and the people gave allegiance to the new caliph.

History would be told that none of the greatest companions would be left without giving allegiance, with the exception of Saad ibn Ubada of the Ansar, the clan of Hashim, and a handful of companions loyal to Ali.

The position of the clan of Hashim could be summed up in two personalities – Ali ibn Abi Talib, and his uncle, Abbas ibn Abd al-Muttalib. Abbas saw Ali as the rightful leader of their people and thus he would not hold a position that opposed Ali's.

There was a group of leading companions who did not give allegiance either and stayed loyal to Ali. Though they were not from Banu Hashim per se, they were grouped with them due to their uncompromising love and loyalty to the Prophet's family. Some of those companions included Salman the Persian, Abuthar al-Ghafari, Miqdad ibn al-Aswad al-Kindi, and Ammar ibn Yassir. History would record these men as the Four Companions, the ones who stayed most loyal to Ali after the Prophet.

Though these companions were not from the elite tribe of Quraysh, they were regarded as the most important companions of God's Prophet. The Prophet adored Salman so much, he considered him to be a member of his own household. Abuthar was praised by the Prophet for his honesty and integrity. Miqdad was promised paradise, and Ammar was honored by the Prophet as a scholar.

These companions were as loyal to Ali as they were to the Prophet, for they saw that a betrayal of such loyalty was a betrayal to the faith that they dedicated their lives to serve. Because of this, the new caliph and his supporters attempted to orchestrate a plan to secure the allegiance of Ali, by any means necessary. If that was achieved, it did not matter whether Saad ibn Ubada and the rest of the Ansar conceded or not.

Abu Bakr gathered his closest advisors – Umar and Abu Ubayda – to discuss the matter and decide the necessary steps moving forward. The two looked at their newly selected leader and waited for some words of action. Instead, they were met with a blank stare that summed up little in emotion or thought. Growing impatient, Umar took the initiative.

"O' Caliph of God's Messenger! You must order them to obey you," Umar exclaimed.

"And if they will not have it?" Abu Bakr asked.

"Then they have caused discord amongst the Muslims, which has consequences," Umar replied.

Abu Ubayda chimed in, "I think you should call Mugheera ibn Shuba, he's a man of worthy opinion."

Thus, they called Mugheera and he came forth to join the conversation. Being filled in on their predicament of how they should go about consolidating power, and effectively lead, given the circumstances, Mugheera shared his thoughts:

"I do not see any way forward but to rip these people apart from one another."

Abu Bakr asked, "And how would we do that?"

"Go to Abbas and tell him that you intend to share power with him, that he and his children shall have part in the caliphate," replied Mugheera.

"Let us say that is done," said Abu Bakr.

"Then you will not face any issues from Ali moving forward."

Abu Bakr took Mugheera's advice. He took Umar with him and went to see Abbas. After their brief greetings, Abu Bakr did not waste much time and brought the subject of power to the forefront. "O' Abbas, you are the leader of this household. We have come to you with the desire to give you a share of this affair, as well as those that come after you from your lineage. For you are the uncle of the Messenger of God..."

Abbas did not allow him to finish his statement. Instead, he interrupted and said, "What you wish to give me, is it your right that you wish to dispense of? Or the right of the believers? Or our right in fact? O' Abu Bakr, if it is your right then keep it for yourself. And if it is the right of the believers, then it is not your place to dispense of it. And if it is our right, then we do not accept to take bits and pieces of it. But what I see is that you have taken the sultanate of Muhammad away from his family and its rightful owners."

"The Messenger of God was from us as much as he was from you, Abbas," Abu Bakr replied, as he tried to mask his irritation.

Abbas smiled and paused for a moment.

"O' Abu Bakr, the Prophet is from a tree, surely we are of its branches, and you are merely its neighbors."

Their attempt failed and they were back at square one. They decided that there was no other way at this point but to directly coerce Ali ibn Abi Talib into paying allegiance. Umar endeavored to talk to Ali and convince him of the matter. But he got nowhere.

Frustrated with Ali's firm position, Umar threatened him and said, "You are not safe until you pay allegiance."

Ali turned around, gave Umar a stern look, and told him to know his place when speaking with him. His threats did not phase Ali, and Umar understood the look that Ali gave him. He went back to Abu Bakr, disappointed once again. Abu Bakr decided to go to Ali and discuss the matter with him diplomatically. Umar and Abu Ubayda would join him for a final attempt in this line of deliberations.

They went to Ali and sat down before him. There was coldness in the room between the hearts that were present. Ali was mourning the loss of his most beloved Muhammad, while the companions were busy trying to figure how to consolidate power in the man they elected to lead instead of Ali.

When Umar was later asked by Abdullah ibn Abbas why he pushed for the election of Abu Bakr, even though he had paid allegiance to Ali at Ghadeer Khum, he offered the following explanation:

> It was out of a cautious concern for the welfare of the Muslims and for the religion of Islam. Quraysh would never have come together under the authority of this young man... They did not want Muhammad's family to rule, since they found it abhorrent to see the prophethood and the caliphate combined in a single family, lest they become overbearing.

That was what Umar argued as his wisdom looking back. Still, the wisdom of the Prophet dictated that Ali was his heir, and no one else. The matter was a decree of God. And yet, these companions of the Prophet presented themselves before Ali to convince him of their own wisdom and their decision to take leadership of the nation into their own hands.

"O' Ali, the people have chosen me to lead them. And I would like to see that you do as the people have done..."

"I am tasked with compiling the Quran and arranging it, before it is neglected or challenged with time... I will not place a robe on my shoulders and leave my home until my task is done," Ali replied poetically.

Abu Bakr did not accept his answer.

Umar was irritated by Ali's eloquent insubordination.

"O' Caliph of God's Messenger, I will make him obey you, for the people have paid you allegiance."

Ali turned to Umar with a disquieting display of anger. He reminded him to know his place, and beware of what his threats would render for his future.

Ali then turned to Abu Bakr and said, "By God, you dressed yourself with the caliphate, and you certainly know that my position in relation to it was the same as the position of the axis to a hand-mill. The flood water flows down from me and the bird cannot fly up to me…"

Umar was about to say something else, but Abu Bakr quickly sent him off, in fear that things would escalate to a point of no return. Abu Bakr changed his demeanor with Ali and pleasantly said, "Do not worry, oh Father of Hasan, if you do not wish to pay allegiance, I will not coerce you."

Abu Bakr then followed Umar out of the room.

Abu Ubayda remained with Ali, in an effort to speak to him in a more diplomatic and appeasing manner, something his friends weren't able to do. The conversation between Ali and Abu Ubayda went on for quite a while, but it was to no avail. The conversation ended with Ali's affirmation of his position. He told him with a voice filled with confidence and certainty:

"By God, it is within us, O' Abu Ubayda. It is within us. Do not follow your whims and stray from the path of God. In that, you will merely increase your distance from the Truth…"

Ali would not leave his stance in supporting the Truth and word of God, and the new administration was at its wits end. They had to get Ali to pay allegiance or their newly established authority would surely be compromised in the eyes of the people. Umar reiterated his readiness to use whatever means necessary to bolster the position of the caliphate.

In the days ahead, he volunteered to go to the house of Ali and force him to pay allegiance to the new caliph. Abu Bakr agreed and sent Umar off with Khaled ibn Waleed and a group of men. The group marched on to the house of Ali and Fatima. On their way, they gathered firewood and brought it with them to the house of Ali.

Upon arriving, they banged on the door and yelled from outside the humble home, calling Ali to come out and give allegiance to the new caliph at the mosque. Ali was in the house with his family and companions. Lady Fatima stood behind the closed door to reply to the people that were banging on her door and harassing her family. Perhaps they would respect her as the grieving daughter of their prophet, who had only just passed away, and leave them be.

She told them they were not welcome in her home and again beseeched the name of their prophet to get them to leave. But that was to no avail. She reminded them of their roots and customs as Arabian men, but how could chivalry even breathe when greed for power filled the air?

Umar began stacking the firewood against the door. Bewildered by the gesture, he was asked by some of his men, "What do you intend on doing with that firewood Umar?"

He turned to his men with a craze in his eyes that brought remnants of *Jahiliya* - the Days of Ignorance of the pre-Islamic era.

"By God, I will burn this house down on him if he does not come out and pay allegiance!"

Umar continued to stack the wood.

"But Fatima is in the house!" one of the men exclaimed.

He replied coldly with only one word.

"So?"

That word alone tells the story that would unfold. Such a story that is too heavy for the heart of Ali. A story of a dark betrayal. Of a darker night. A blessed body laid to rest by only the light of the moon and the tears of Ali. A story that will be told, recalling his last whispered words to her blessed soul, "Loss of a beloved is exile…".

CHAPTER 13

AFTER SUNSET

Gazing at Ali is worship.

– Muhammad

Lady Fatima passed away less than three months after her father, the Prophet of God. Ali was heartbroken. The two most beloved people in his life were now gone. The pain he endured was like the Prophet when he himself lost the two most beloved people to him, his wife Khadija and his uncle Abu Talib, years earlier. The Prophet named that year *Aam al-Huzn* – the Year of Sorrow. For Ali, the sorrow after the deaths of his brother Muhammad and his wife Fatima was unbearable. The death of Fatima left him as a young father of four small children – Hasan, Husayn, Zaynab, and Um Kulthum. The immeasurable love of Ali, however, carried his children and lit their path like a full moon in the night's sky. He raised his children to be pious scholars and servant leaders, just like the Prophet raised him with his warmth, care, and love.

It was that love that carried and protected the nation after Muhammad. The Prophet was the *Habeeb Allah* – the Beloved of God – and Ali was his heir. Though he did not assume the caliphate, he would still be the unequivocal leader of the

Prophet's people. The heir of the Prophet cared for the hearts, the minds, and the souls of the people. For that, Ali did not fight for power. It was beneath him to do so.

After the death of Fatima, Ali and his companions acquiesced to the new caliphate, and suspended their apparent opposition to the new government. Some may have been perplexed by this; others saw it clearly. Why now did they acquiesce, and what would that mean for the future of Islam and the Muslims?

Ali would share with his companions the clear instructions that the Prophet gave him before he passed:

> The Messenger of God told me, 'If they gather against you, do what I have commanded you. Stay your chest to the ground.' When they deviated away from me, I [persevered] despite the adversity. I closed my eyelids and endured the pricking in my eyes. I stayed my chest to the ground....

It would be as if Ali saw two options in front of him: one, to revolt against the new political establishment, or two, to remain patient. He saw patience as accepting the reality before him and focusing on his ultimate goal of protecting the faith. Ali's love for Islam was far too great and his vision too strong to not see a friend in patience. Ultimately, that is the path that he chose, even though it required him to sacrifice his own rights. Ali would say,

> I will remain patient, until even patience tires of my patience.

Even though the sanctity of his home was violated and dishonored, he bit his tongue and carried on. Ali's sole interest was protecting Islam and serving the Prophet of God. He chose patience over everything else, because it was the only way to fulfill his godly mission – to protect the honor of the Prophet and his Message, and to spread God's justice for all people.

The "allegiance" that the clan of Hashim gave to the caliphate was not one based in faith and conviction of the caliph's legitimacy. Instead, they were functionally coerced into paying homage to the new caliph. It was quickly established that violence would be exercised with those who refused to pay allegiance to the caliphate. No one was safe, not even the closest people to the Prophet. The attack on the house of Ali and Fatima made that very clear.

The intelligent realized that coercion makes any contract or statement invalid. Such coercion was seen throughout history, and the protectors of faith have always been in sensitive and difficult positions. As the family of the Prophet and the protectors of the religion, Banu Hashim saw that fighting in those moments was not only an unwise option, but could lead to the destruction of the religion of God. Ali's individual right to the caliphate, though it was sanctioned by the Prophet, was outweighed by the risk levied by the free will of individuals who yearned for power and position.

The reality is that Ali did not have enough supporters to choose the first option of defending his rights by force. The people in his corner were a small handful of loyal companions. They were ready to give their lives for his cause, but there were just too few in number to effectively rise against the oppression they faced. Ali said,

If I had forty men of will, I would have risen.

In the interest of the preservation of Islam, Ali and his men patiently observed the status quo and did not pursue an aggressive opposition to the establishment. Instead, he remained connected to the center of the caliphate. He did not isolate himself from the affairs of the nation. Though Ali did not assume any official or formal role in government, he was often turned to for his wisdom and knowledge. When it came to ethics, religion, and legal matters, the caliphate sought out Ali for his advice and counsel. Advise he did and counsel he was. Ali's priority was to safeguard the principles and teachings of the Prophet, so that the nation would not veer off more than it already had from the straight path.

Ali was the leading jurist of his time – the highest scholar and judge, deciding the affairs of the people in times of conflict and dispute. His position would be so essential that the man who would become the second caliph only two years after the first would say, "If it were not for Ali, I would have perished."

Ali and the few men in his company did not acquiesce until after the death of Fatima. It was not merely out of respect for her; rather, with the death of Fatima came silence of truth. The reality was that Fatima was Ali's champion. She was his true advocate, and the only one who could demand for his rights while preserving the body of Islam and its sanctity. After she died, that voice of truth was suppressed, and Ali was left all alone.

For this reason, he had no other choice but to acquiesce to the new caliphate, to avoid any further bloodshed or defiling of the sanctity of Islam.

With all this, Ali still took the opportunity to articulate his position to those in his midst every chance he got. Though he chose patience and even advised those who had taken rule into their own hands, he was not silent to those who changed the course of history.

The reign of the first caliph would last for two years and three months before Abu Bakr would die. Ali was distant from the course of events that took place in its earliest days, as he was busy further compiling the Holy Quran and teaching his followers and companions. It is said that the Quran had been completely revealed and its verses compiled in their respected chapters by the Prophet before he passed. Ali was tasked by the Prophet to organize the order of its chapters thereafter.

When the seditions and instigations began to take place, like the Ridda wars, in which some groups rebelled against the state, Ali got involved without hesitation. Regardless of all that had happened, and all that was in Ali's heart of pain and anguish, he kept it inside and looked at the greater good. People needed security, the nation was to be preserved, and the religion defended.

Ali spoke of this ordeal and expressed his thoughts on the matter clearly:

> By God, it never occurred to me, and I never imagined, that after the Prophet, the Arabs would snatch away the caliphate from his Household, nor that they would take it away from

me after him, but I suddenly noticed people surrounding the man to swear him allegiance.

I therefore withheld my hand till I saw that many people were reverting from Islam and trying to destroy the religion of Muhammad. I then feared that if I did not protect Islam and its people, and there occurred in it a breach or destruction, it would mean a greater blow to me than the loss of power over you which was, in any case, to last for a few days of which everything would pass away, as the mirage passes away, or as the cloud scuds away. Therefore, in these happenings, I rose till wrong was destroyed and disappeared, and religion attained peace and safety.

Ali would command his own companions to dress in their armor and prepare their swords for battle at any moment. This was not to demand his own rights, but to defend the faith from the dangers of those wishing to cause bloodshed at the Battle of Yamama. Though they threatened the caliphate of Abu Bakr directly, it was also a threat on the body of Islam. The faith could not be compromised – that was Ali's highest priority. In the public's eye, Ali was dedicated to compiling the Quran, educating his people, directing an intellectual movement, and maintaining civility and unity within the nation. Even though he was personally wronged, and his rights usurped, he sacrificed those rights to protect the body of Islam and the wellbeing of the nation. He loved Islam too much, cared for its people too deeply, to be distracted from his highest goals.

Ali ibn Abi Talib was critical in matters of jurisprudence and judgment in the courts of the caliphate. Abu Bakr leaned on him to ensure that the proper judgments were made in his court, especially with more complex matters of religion and society.

During Abu Bakr's short tenure, a man was brought before his court to be punished for drinking wine. The man pleaded, "I drank it not knowing that it was prohibited. I was brought amongst people who did not forbid it."

Not knowing how to judge on the matter, Abu Bakr called on Ali to advise him. Thus, Ali directed him as follows:

> Have two trustworthy men from amongst the Muslims take him to the gatherings of the Muhajiroun and the Ansar. Let them ask if anyone amongst them recited to this man the verse of prohibition, or a narration from the Prophet speaking to the matter. If two men could bear witness that he was informed, then give him his punishment. But if the witnesses are not established, the let him go...'

The Caliph did as Ali directed him. No one could testify that the man was informed and knew of the prohibition of wine. Thus, his life was spared, and he was set free.

Abu Bakr expressed his appreciation for Ali's position with the caliphate and said, "Whoever wishes to see the closest people to the Messenger of God, the highest in status, the greatest in tribulation, and the most superior amongst you then he should look at him," Abu Bakr pointed to Ali. "He is compassionate with people and patient with what comes to him."

Though it seems contradictive in the personality and character of Abu Bakr to have assumed the caliphate as he did, but at the same time admire Ali, it was a reality experienced by most. Regardless of people's political position with Ali ibn Abi Talib, even those who later waged war on him and fought him in battle, they could not help but admire him, and be in awe of his virtuous personality.

Like many of the companions of the Prophet, Abu Bakr used to stare at the face of Ali ibn Abi Talib with awe and adoration. His daughter, Aisha, noticed that. Puzzled, she asked him why he did that.

Abu Bakr replied, "How could I not? When the Prophet himself said, 'Gazing at Ali is worship.'"

CHAPTER 14

THE SECOND CALIPHATE

If it were not for Ali, I would have perished.

– Umar ibn Al-Khattab

The era of Umar arrived. Though his predecessor only ruled for a little over two years, Umar would rule for a whole decade. And though his predecessor came to rule by the election of a select group of his peers, Umar was appointed by the caliph himself. His appointment was not done in secret or with any bashfulness: it was clear and straightforward declaration by his comrade – "Umar is the caliph after me."

The people who elected the first caliph were still alive, and therefore many of them were left bewildered. Why would the matter of the caliphate not be brought before them once again so they may determine the fate of their people?

Soon after his appointment as the next caliph and Abu Bakr's heir-apparent, one of the companions sat next to Umar in a gathering. The companion turned to Umar with a smug smile. "You crowned him yesterday, and he crowned you today," he scoffed.

Abd al-Rahman ibn Aouf would go to Abu Bakr himself on his deathbed and tell him, "O' Abu Bakr, we see that you have appointed Umar to rule over us… and you know him and how he is amongst us. You're about to meet your Lord, and he will ask you about this, so what will you say?"

The response was silence.

The questioning and bewilderment quickly diminished. Umar took control and established his authority across the Muslim lands. In fact, he broadened Muslim control through conquest and calls for holy war to expand the Muslim Empire.

People were busied with conquest, a thriving economy, and the new cultures and experiences that came along with it. The nation was growing at a rapid speed. Riches were being accumulated. Glory of conquest apparent. So, where was Ali in all of this?

Ali was hard at work. He did not stop his day-to-day jobs in earning an honest living. At the same time, he was committed to his school of students to disseminate the holy knowledge entrusted to him by his beloved brother, Prophet Muhammad.

His students would spread themselves across the communities of the nation to be pillars of knowledge and trust that the people could lean on. Ali's days were long and his nights short, as he stayed awake resolving matters of the state from within, and working to ensure the nation was protected from both its external and internal threats. Ali worked alongside anyone who wanted good for the nation, and served the people.

The caliph knew very well the position of Banu Hashim when it came to the caliphate. He knew that they reserved their right to the caliphate, and presumed that one day they would demand their right to rule, if the circumstances allowed for it. Thus, he made sure that they would be far from any public positions of authority or influence where they could rally the masses around them. He especially made this so for their leader – Ali ibn Abi Talib. Still, he kept Ali near his court and chambers, as well as within his circle of advisors, as the first caliph had done.

Though Umar had said his famous line on multiple occasions, "If it were not for Ali, I would have perished," he could not risk having Ali's personality and charisma gain any traction of influence with the masses. Ali was seen as a political opponent, one with a different philosophy of leadership and an agenda that differed substantially from his own.

Umar would go the length to ensure Ali was not seen as superior to his peers in position or leadership, even after Umar's death. After reaching the ten-year mark of his reign as caliph, Umar was attacked in an assassination attempt on his life. His wounds were fatal and his end near.

Umar appointed a council of six companions, whom he nominated for the caliphate. The council was to choose amongst themselves who was to be the next Caliph of the Muslims. The council included Talhah ibn Ubaydallah, Zubayr ibn Al-Awwam, Uthman ibn Affan, Saad ibn Abi Waqqas, Abd al-Rahman ibn Aouf, and Ali ibn Abi Talib.

Such a move naturally put Ali at a disadvantage in the public eye. By the caliph's appointment amongst these five other candidates, Ali was not seen as special or superior. He was not seen as the one; instead, he was merely one among six.

Umar outlined the process and procedure by which this council would elect among themselves the next caliph. The decision was to be made by majority – majority rules. If there is a deadlock, with three on one side and three on the other, then the side that Abd al-Rahman ibn Aouf was on would win in its decision. Finally, if they did not reach a decision within three days of commencement, they would all be executed by order of the state.

From the outset, it was clear that Uthman was the caliphate's choice. The dynamic between the council could only lead to that result. Abd al-Rahman was Uthman's brother-in-law. Saad ibn Abi Waqqas was Abd al-Rahman's cousin, and he would not oppose him in whatever decision he made. Talhah would never choose someone from Banu Hashim. So that left Zubayr, who, even if he leaned towards Ali, it would not mean anything, because the scales ultimately tipped toward Uthman and no one else.

"O' Ali, I know that if you were to rule over them, you would do so with a justice so vivid, and a proof so pure, and you would take them on the straight path," Umar would say to Ali. What is peculiar is what he said of to the five remaining members of the council.

"I would have chosen you, Abd al-Rahman but you are the Pharaoh of this nation."

"Your tribalism and nepotism deter me from you," Umar would say to Uthman.

"If I were to crown Talhah, he would dress the ring of the caliphate on the hand of his woman."

"And what precludes me from appointing you, Saad, is your harshness and your heart of stone."

"As for you Zubayr, you are a believer when you are pleased, but become an apostate when you are angered."

CHAPTER 15

UTHMAN & THE RISE OF UMAYYA

O' Sons of Umayya! Pass the caliphate to each other, one after the other!

– Abu Sufyan

"It is as if Quraysh has given you this matter, and through it, you would make Banu Umayya and Bani Abi Mu'eet a chain around people's necks. Until they will not be able to take it anymore, and a band of Arabian wolves will come for you and slaughter you as you sleep in your bed…" Those were the words of Umar to Uthman before he passed.

Indeed, his words would prove true. Uthman would rule for twelve years, longer than both his predecessors did. His more than a decade-long reign would be characterized by a revival of tribalism, nepotism, and corruption in the empire. Because of that, the people's confidence in the circle of advisors and governors around the caliph seriously diminished.

When Uthman assumed the caliphate, the Umayyads filled the house of Uthman. The chief and eldest of the Umayyads, Abu Sufyan, entered the gathering. Being blind at the time, he was helped to a seat where he could be heard and seen. Before speaking he asked, "Is there anyone other than the Umayyads here?"

"Speak with ease, Abu Sufyan," they reassured him.

His chest became broader and he bellowed with revenge, "O' Sons of Umayya! Pass the caliphate to each other, one after the other! By the one that Abu Sufyan swears by, I still desire it for you, and it shall be for your sons! For by God, there is no Heaven and there is no Hell..."

In the house of the new caliph, these words were not opposed, or met with any apprehension. Uthman did not stop the old man or follow up Abu Sufyan's blasphemy with a correcting statement of belief or piety. Instead, he nodded as all the sons of Umayya did. Their time had come and nothing was to stand in their way.

Abu Sufyan was the first archenemy of the Prophet of Islam. He swore to fight the Prophet and everything he stood for so long as air filled his lungs. He was counted amongst the nobles of Quraysh who waged most of the wars and battles against Islam and the Muslims.

Now, twenty years later, Abu Sufyan would stand over the grave of Hamza ibn Abd al-Muttalib with spite and cowardly revenge. Hamza was the one of the bravest of Islam's warriors, sometimes even called the Lion of God and His Prophet. Hamza would tragically fall martyr in the Battle of Uhud.

Abu Sufyan stood over Hamza's grave, rubbed his feet in its sand, and said, "Rise O' Hamza, and see how the dominion you fought us over has become in the hands of our boys!"

When Uthman came to power, he appointed new governors, advisors, and aides of the state for his new administration. Most of them, if not all of them, came from two tribes – Umayya and Abi Mu'eet.

These new aides were especially not cognizant or observant of Islamic customs and mannerisms that were expected as representatives of the state. They were openly immoral and unashamedly displayed depravity.

Waleed ibn 'Uqba ibn Abi Mu'eet was appointed by Uthman as the new governor of Kufa. Before being appointed, he had left the religion of Islam, and at some point, he accepted the faith again. One night, he had a gathering in his home that lasted until the break of dawn. For hours, he and his guests drank, ate, and laughed the night away.

When the time of prayer came at the strike of dawn, he was called to lead the people in prayer. He went out to the mosque, still wearing the night clothes he got drunk in, and began prayers. Though the prayer was only to be performed in two units of standing and prostration, Waleed prayed eight. At the conclusion of his eighth rik'aa, or unit of prayer, he turned around to the people behind him.

"I can add some more if you'd like," he said with a drunken smile.

The entire character of the Muslim state was changing. Beyond corruption that could be covered up and done behind the scenes, there were blatant displays of betrayal and insult to the memory of their Grand Prophet. Al-Hakam ibn Abi Al-Aas was appointed as a government official and given one hundred thousand dirhams, even though he was exiled by the Holy Prophet.

Al-Harath ibn Al-Hakam was given a large market in Medina, which was previously an endowment established by the Prophet for needy and destitute Muslims. Marwan ibn Al-Hakam was given the land of Fadak, which was the inherited property of the Prophet's daughter, Our Lady Fatima. To add insult to injury, Marwan was given one hundred thousand dirhams from the public treasury.

Abu Sufyan was given two hundred thousand dirhams from the treasury of the Muslims. The revenues collected from the provinces of Iraq were distributed amongst the nobles of Banu Umayya. The jewels and rubies of the state's treasury deposited during the reign of Umar were withdrawn and gifted to the daughters of Uthman.

The Al-Hakam family were such a danger on the nation during the lifetime of the Prophet that he exiled them to the land of Ta'if. Al-Shaykhan (the first two caliphs) heeded to the Prophet's directives on this matter, and would not dare to bring them back into the fold of society.

Uthman, on the other hand, had the boldness not only to bring them back, but to pay them from the state treasury, and appoint Marwan ibn Al-Hakam to his cabinet as a top advisor.

The third caliph and his administration had an audacious disregard of the Prophet's companions, such as Abuthar Al-Ghafari, Ammar ibn Yasser, and Abdullah ibn Mas'oud. On one occasion, Abuthar was in the presence of Uthman, discussing matters of the state. Abuthar did not hesitate to criticize and show the faults in Uthman's debauched policies and depraved politics.

Infuriated by Abuthar's criticisms, Uthman exiled him to Syria. Uthman ordered his governor there, Muawiya ibn Abu Sufyan, to punish him accordingly. Muawiya was building his own political profile, and did not want his reputation tainted with punishing one of the Prophet's closest companions in public. Thus, he sent word back to Uthman and asked to be excused from the task.

"There is no one more truthful in all of these lands than Abuthar," were the words of the Holy Prophet.

Still, Uthman chose to have him exiled to Al-Rabadhah, deep into the deserts of Arabia, to die lonely and estranged.

Ammar ibn Yasser was also dealt with for his courage. He would demand that the caliph reform his policies and bring the nation back on to the straight path of Islam. Appalled by his audacity to make such demands, Uthman looked to his advisor, Marwan ibn Al-Hakam, on what punishment to give Ammar for his insolence.

The Holy Prophet told his companion, "O' Ammar, the transgressors will kill you…" Marwan advised Uthman to order his execution, and relieve the Umayyads of his nuisance.

Instead, Uthman ordered his men to beat him to a pulp. The honorable companion was manhandled by the caliph's guards and beaten senselessly. Uthman would get up from his throne and join them in beating Ammar until he became unconscious.

"Throw him out on the street," Uthman ordered his men.

There lay one of the closest companions to the Prophet of Islam, bruised from head to toe, and stretched out on the streets of the capital. Um Salama, the widow of the Prophet, heard of the news and sent some young men to carry Ammar and bring him to her home. For hours he lay unconscious, until he finally awoke after sunset.

"Praise be to God," were the words he uttered as he opened his eyes. Gaining consciousness, he realized he had missed his daily prayers. After he made up his prayers, Ammar said in a low voice,

"Though I have been beaten and tortured, so long as it is in the way of God, I am fine..."

Abdullah ibn Mas'oud had a confrontation with Uthman at the mosque. After they exchanged some words, Uthman ordered for him to be kicked out of the mosque and beaten. Abdullah was shocked and refused to leave the mosque.

The mosque was the ultimate sanctuary as the house of God, and no one could kick him out of the house of God. But to no avail, Uthman repeated the order to his men and they obliged. Chaos erupted in the mosque, but it was quickly quelled by the state's guards. Abdullah resisted, and was beaten even more severely for it.

He was delivered to his home with too many broken bones to count. His home was forbidden from any aid or medical assistance. He was left to die. Days later, his time came and Abdullah passed on to the next abode. Before he died, he asked Ammar to pray over his body and bury him in secret.

The situation continued to get worse as the new administration's heavy-handed policies disgruntled so many of the public. The government's unbashful approach to politics, along with their abusiveness to those who were not part of their class or tribe, could only be tolerated for so long. People were outraged.

Other companions and well-respected individuals in the community of Muslims became more vocal. Such individuals included Talhah, Zubayr, and even Aisha – "the Mother of the Believers," a title attributed to the wives of the Prophet.

Aisha released a *fatwa*, or verdict, that said plainly, "Kill the Hyena, for he has disbelieved."

Abd al-Rahman ibn Aouf, Uthman's greatest ally and catalyst for his coming to the throne, would come to say in his later years, "If I had the foresight to see what I now see in hindsight, I would not have given Uthman authority even over my shoe."

"Get him out! Get him out! Before his power expands any further!" were the words Abd al-Rahman repeated on his deathbed before he passed. In his will, he specifically requested that anyone but Uthman pray on his body when the time of his death came.

So where was Ali in all of this?

As always, his priority was safeguarding the body of Islam. The faith and its people had to be protected. Even when others had their aims elsewhere, he could not stray. He would not.

Ali was very upfront and straightforward with Uthman throughout his reign, but he knew how to get the point across and maintain the peace. He provided constructive criticism and did not hold back from illustrating the right path forward, whether it was in politics and policy, finances and the treasury, or judgment and the court system.

Whatever was in conflict with the Book of God and the tradition of the Prophet, Ali would clearly point it out, and show the way to correct what was wrong. But Ali's counsel could only go so far when Uthman surrounded himself with the likes of Abu Sufyan and Marwan ibn Al-Hakam.

When the day of Abuthar's exile came, the caliph ordered that no one was to see him off. Ali, however, insisted on seeing Abuthar before he was sent off to Al-Rabadhah. He brought his sons Hasan and Husayn, his brother Aqeel, along with Ammar ibn Yasser.

Marwan tried to prevent them from getting close to Abuthar by standing in their way. Ali responded to Marwan harshly and told him to leave at once. Marwan left and immediately informed Uthman of what happened. The caliph took offense to the incident and reprimanded Ali upon his return.

Ali defended his position to Uthman, and insisted that the caliphate cannot order transgression, nor can he stand in the way of fulfilling a moral duty. And if the caliphate were to assume such a role, then such a caliphate would not be respected and could not be followed. Uthman did not concede to his position and asserted that he took personal insult to Ali's actions.

After some silence, Uthman asked Ali to apologize to Marwan for defying Uthman's orders, and for disrespecting Marwan as his agent. Marwan stood there smugly awaiting Ali's apology. Unmoved by the request, Ali respectfully refused.

If we were flies on the most distant wall of the caliphate's chambers, we could see the stand-off between two extraordinarily different men. On one side, you had Marwan ibn Al-Hakam, and on the other side there was Ali ibn Abi Talib. Marwan was the son of the disgraced exiled enemy of God's Prophet. But Marwan was Uthman's cousin.

Aisha on one occasion told Marwan, "I heard the Messenger of God tell your father and your grandfather, Abi Al-Aas ibn Umayya, that your family is the damned tree mentioned in the Quran."

On the other hand, Ali was the one whom the Prophet described in this way: "Ali is with the Truth, and the Truth is with Ali. It turns with him wherever he may go." The caliph could not distinguish between truth and falsehood, between good and evil; instead he was overcome by passion and the mere thought of his word being defied enflamed him.

"Why will you not apologize to him Ali? Are you better than him?!"

But Ali would remain as he was, that unwavering citadel of Islam. Though Uthman was quick to forget, Ali was not. And even as the time would come and Uthman would need Ali more than ever, Ali would not rub it in his face and leave him to the wolves. Ali's loyalty, honor, and faith would be shown when things only became worse for the caliphate.

Delegations from Egypt, Kufa, Basra and other parts of the empire came to the capital demanding reform in the nation. They came in such great numbers, that it looked more and more like a revolution, rather than a few delegates from the corners of the empire. The people were rising and so Uthman ran to the only person who knew how to handle the situation – Ali.

"I spoke to you on more than one occasion and warned you of this. The nation needs reform. You did not heed to my advice, rather you continued to do what you were doing. Indeed, that was from Marwan, Muawiya, Ibn Amer, and Abdullah ibn Saad. You followed them and disavowed me."

"You have my word, I will concede. I will implement reform," Uthman promised Ali.

But as soon as the storm passed, Uthman reverted back to his old ways. His clansmen continued to take advantage of the current state, and the reforms that were promised never came to fruition. The storm returned, and Ali remained. Ali was that intermediary force that kept both sides at bay. With the rebels on one side, and Uthman and his caliphate on the other, Ali was the eye of the storm.

Ali was beseeched by both sides, and in turn was required to meet with multiple parties. Whenever he met with Uthman, the rebels accused him of being loyal to the caliphate. When he spoke to the rebels, the followers of Uthman would whisper in the ears of the caliph and cause trouble between him and Ali.

But despite all of this, Ali remained focused on resolutions and reform. To protect the welfare of the state and keep the peace, Ali would even order his own sons, Hasan and Husayn, to dress in their battle gear and protect the house of Uthman. It was a clear message that mutiny of this kind would not serve the nation, and that the body of Islam had to be protected, no matter what the cost.

Ali would go on to avert the rebels' plot to assassinate Uthman. That night, they were meeting in the house of Talhah, conspiring on how to kill the caliph. Ali went to the state treasury and had the chests opened. He ordered those in the treasury to have sums of money brought forth and distributed to the people.

The rebels in the house of Talhah got wind of the news and hurried to the treasury to get their share, leaving their plots and schemes behind them. Talhah was left all alone.

With his head down in shame, he walked over to Uthman to apologize for his indiscretion. "I ask God for forgiveness and repent to him before you. I desired something but God prevented it from happening…"

"By God, you did not come here in repentance, rather you came here in defeat. God is your judge," Uthman replied.

But there was only so much harm Ali could ward off, and only so much time he could buy for Uthman. Hearing of the possibility of reinforcements from Syria sent by Muawiya to save the besieged caliph, the rebels finally stormed the house of Uthman. They found the old caliph sitting with his wife, Naila, some say reciting Quran in his final hours. Seeing them seated on the floor reading the holy book, the rebels did not flinch. It was a purge of grievances and a craze of vengeance expressed by the thrashing of their swords on his frail body. Though Naila survived with injuries, Uthman did not stand a chance. His blood covered the room, and his soul departed his body. With his murder, Uthman's twelve-year reign finally came to an end and the rebels saw in that a victory, albeit brief. So where would the nation go now?

CHAPTER 16

THE PEOPLE'S CHAMPION

You know who Ali is and I do not know of anyone more capable of this matter or more qualified.

– Ammar ibn Yasser

The storm did not entirely end with the murder of Uthman. Dark clouds still loomed above. The rebels sheathed their swords, and the Muslims called out to the people of Medina. "O' People of Medina, you are the people of the council and you tie the knot of leadership. Your decision is binding on the nation. So, choose a man and we will follow."

From every direction, near and far, the people called out one name. A name that echoed from the mountains and through the valleys. A name that washed over and soothed a nation that had endured years of oppression and injustice, reigniting hope on its horizons. A name that brought ease to the hearts and minds, and that once uttered truth was known. That name was Ali.

"Ali! Ali ibn Abi Talib! We are pleased with him!"

The fact of the matter was that there truly was no one else more qualified than he, in such a way that no one had a shadow of doubt that he indeed was the most fit to lead.

Ammar ibn Yasser would rise and speak to the masses of people in Medina:

> O' Ansar, Uthman was amongst you yesterday and you were witnesses... and today you may fall into the same experience if you are not wary. And you know that Ali is the foremost of people in this matter, for his virtue and experience. O' Muhajiroun, you know who Ali is, and I do not know of anyone more capable of this matter or more qualified.

Ali was not distant from the people. He lived amongst them throughout the decades of change and turmoil. More than anyone, his faith and solidarity was tested. The people saw his struggles and witnessed his patience. For that, they knew there was no better option to place their fate in.

"We accept, for he is to us as you mentioned and even better..."

The people took to the house of Ali to pay their allegiance to their man of choice. They gathered around his humble home and waited for him to come out and greet them. Ali opened the door and was met with cheers by the people. The cheers finally quieted down, and one of the men stepped forward to say,

"O' Ali, the man has been killed, and the people cannot be without a leader. We do not see anyone more deserving than you in this matter. No one is, or has been, closer to the Messenger of God than you."

Ali looked at the scores of men before him. He saw the hope in their faces. He also saw the circumstances that had befallen them. He refused to take advantage of them.

"There is no need for me in this matter. I am with you. For whoever you choose, I am pleased with…"

The masses did not accept his refusal. They could not.

"We beseech you by God! Do you not see what we see? Have you not seen what has happened in Islam? Do you not see the sedition upon us? Do you not fear God?"

Their voices only got louder, and more and more men shouted the pain that lay in their hearts. That pain could only be healed by the one who was a remedy for their souls. There was one Amir amongst them – a prince who serves the people in the way of God, and that was Ali. They urged him to take the caliphate. The men were adamant on convincing him in this matter, even though they knew it was not going to be an easy feat.

Though yesterday, the nation may have stood in his way, today they stood for him. And with their choice to stand by his side, they chose a man who loves God and His Prophet and whom God and His Prophet love.

After seeing that they were not going to budge on their nomination of him, Ali reemphasized his position:

Leave me and seek someone else. We are facing a matter with several options and many preferences. You call for change that hearts are unready to stand, and minds are unwilling to accept. Clouds are hovering overhead. The path has disguised itself. You should know that if I respond to you, I would lead you as I know I should lead. I would not listen to the utterance of any speaker or the reproach of any admonisher. If you leave me then I am the same as you are. In fact, I may be the one who listens best and obeys whomever you make in charge of your affairs. I am better for you as a counselor than as chief.

The uproar reignited and the men called out in unison, "We will not leave you, until we pay allegiance to you!"

With the calm of the heart of a believer Ali would respond to the people.

"If you wish for this, then it shall take place in the mosque. Allegiance to me shall not be made in private, it will only be done in public and before the masses."

The people gathered in the Mosque of the Prophet. Their eyes were glued to the gates of the Mosque as they waited for Ali to walk through. Moments later, he arrived. His prestige was undeniable, and people gazed at his stature in awe.

"O' people, this is your matter. No one has right in it except those whom you choose. We have parted ways in the past. If you wish, I will settle for you, for I do not see anyone else for this matter…"

The crowd replied, "Yes, we are here for what we missed in the past."

"Except that I did not wish to rule over you. But you refused and were adamant that I lead you…"

Their voices grew louder again, "We pledge allegiance to you by the Book of God!"

Ali raised his hands to the Heavens in those moments and said, "My Lord be witness over them."

The people rushed over to Ali to pay homage as their new caliph.

The day after the people paid allegiance to Ali, it was announced that Ali was going to give a sermon to the people to outline his platform and agenda. The mosque was so full that people were practically sitting on top of one another. As Ali walked in, the noise reduced to a calm. They watched their leader ascend the pulpit. After he began in God's highest name, with all his glory and praise, Ali spoke to the people:

> Oh people, I am one of you – I have the same rights and bear the same responsibilities. I will rule amongst you in the method of your Prophet and will carry out his commands. By God, every tract of land granted by Uthman or any wealth that he gave out of public treasure will be returned to the treasury. Justice cannot be obstructed by anything. Even if I find that by such money, women have been married or slaves have been purchased, I would confiscate it. Justice will be ample. He who finds it hard to act justly should find it harder to deal with injustice.

Certainly, those men who were immersed in the pleasures of this world – they amassed estates, dug rivers, rode thoroughbred horses, and assembled beautiful maidens, to which this became shame and a disgrace – if I were to deprive them of what excess they enjoyed, and gave them what they know to be the extent of their right, they would say, 'the son of Abu Talib has deprived us of our rights!'

Surely, if any of the companions of the Messenger of God, whether of the Muhajiroun or the Ansar, sees that he is better than others because of his companionship with the Prophet – he should know that preference is given in the hereafter by God. Your reward and recompense are with God. And surely, anyone who answered the call of God and His Messenger, believed in our teachings, entered our faith, and faced our Qibla [in worship] has deserved the rights of Islam and its responsibilities.

You are the servants of God, and all wealth belongs to Him. So, the public wealth will be divided amongst you equally. No one shall have any preference over another. The pious shall receive their increased rewards, and the best of recompense from God in the hereafter. God did not make the material world a reward or recompense for the pious, and what God holds [for the hereafter] is better for the righteous.

When tomorrow comes, come back to us. We have money that must be split amongst the public. None of you should stay back, regardless of whether you are an Arab or a non-Arab, and whether you were apportioned from the treasury before or not..."

Ali laid out his political platform and agenda for financial reform in his new government. He wished to reform the policies that had previously reinforced societal classes, disenfranchised minorities, and delivered plain injustice. His policies would be based on fairness, justice, and equality. This alone was enough to ignite sedition and instigation in a nation that, for many years had become accustomed to a lifestyle that was anything but characteristic of justice and equality.

The next day, the people gathered at the treasury's door. Ali told his scribe Ubaidallah ibn Abi Rafi, "Begin with the Muhajiroun and call them to receive their portion. Give each of them three dinars. Then call the Ansar and give them all the same amount. Do the same with everyone that comes to you – whether he is white or black."

Sahl ibn Honaif, a known aristocrat, objected, saying, "This man was my slave yesterday and I only freed him today."

Ali replied, "We will give him as we give you."

Each of them was given three dinars.

No one was given preference over any other. There were only a handful of individuals who did not attend and receive their share, including Talha, Zubayr, Abdullah ibn Umar, Saeed ibn Al-Aas, and Marwan ibn Al-Hakam, amongst others from Quraysh and other tribes.

Some of those around Ali suggested possibly easing up on the execution of some of these economic policies, as to lighten the blowback from the elites in the nation. They were not used to this kind of justice and it was hard to do away with the class system they had known so well enforced by the previous administrations. People could not handle all of this change all at once, they argued. But Ali's position was unwavering. He responded to them firmly:

"Do you ask me to seek favor through injustice to those whom I have been given authority over? By God, I would not even come close to such action so long as time goes on, and as long as one star follows the other in the sky. If this money was mine, I would divide it equitably. How do you ask me to be inequitable when this wealth belongs to God?"

For Ali, his interest was not in gaining the favor of the elites. Instead, he wished to protect the rights of the poor and downtrodden. The instances of Ali's commitment to this egalitarian style of governance are plenty.

One day, as he did from time to time, Ali walked through the marketplace. Though he was the caliph, he did not fancy an entourage and grand appearances. Instead, he walked amongst the people as one of them. Dressed in plain clothes, Ali comfortably walked through the marketplace. That day, however, he witnessed something that truly troubled him, He saw an old blind man begging. The poor man went from one person to the next asking for help.

"Please help me," the beggar quietly asked one man. "Do you have anything to aid me with?" he asked another.

Not a single person stopped to help the old man. Outraged, Imam Ali looked at the people around him and exclaimed, "Who is this?" In other words, "Why is this man being ignored by you all?"

One man responded simply, "He is a Christian."

The color in Ali's face changed.

"How dare you! You used him up in his youth until he grew old, and now in his old age, unable to work, you neglect him and cut him off?" Ali reprimanded. His voice echoed across the busy stands of the marketplace.

The bazaar went quiet. Everyone stopped.

"Send word to the treasury and have this man's needs met," Ali commanded.

Imam Ali would not leave the market until that elderly Christian man was cared for in every way. He would not rest until anyone that crossed his path with a need or request was indeed fulfilled. The life of Ali tells of how he spent his days and nights during his rule. In the day, he fought for jus-tice in government, in the marketplace, and on the battlefield. At night, he went from home to home in the neighborhoods of his city, leaving baskets of food and sweets at the doors of the downtrodden and less fortunate. He was veiled by a hooded cape in addition to the darkness of the night. The scores of less fortunate families that received these gifts did not know it was Ali, until the baskets stopped arriving after he breathed his last.

Ali's love for Islam, his servitude to the Almighty, and loyalty to the Holy Prophet's mission made him resilient in the face of opposition. No matter the odds against him, his principles did not waver. Thus, his reforms for justice in pursuit of a true egalitarian society continued.

CHAPTER 17

FAITH AND JUSTICE

I do not double-deal in matters of my faith and I will not be compromised by the wretched.

– Ali

A new storm thundered in the face of Ali's caliphate. This storm was unlike any other. It did not merely wish to flaunt rage or fury. This storm desired utter annihilation.

What the clans of Quraysh had feared twenty-five years ago finally came to reality. The first three caliphates gave their clans a distinction of political leadership after the Prophet. Banu Tameem, Banu Adi, and Banu Umayya enjoyed this. But none of them were as distinguished as Banu Hashim, for both the Prophethood and the caliphate graced this one house.

This was intolerable to the chiefs of Quraysh and the resentment that showed in the past manifested itself once again.

Of course, this was not the only factor that brought about the storm. The new administration of Ali ibn Abi Talib had a mission – establishing the standard of just governance and promoting an egalitarian society. Ali's mission created policies of economic, political, and social reform that shook the status quo and worried the wealthy and powerful.

Ali's egalitarian approach leveled the playing field and created an atmosphere of equal opportunity and access to resources, regardless of race, ethnicity, or tribe. Though this empowered the previously disenfranchised groups of the nation, it was not pleasing to the class of people who had tremendously benefited from the one-sided policies of the past.

In the eyes of God, all men are created equal. Social status, family name, wealth or any other fabricated distinguisher in society has no bearing on the quality of an individual. Ali wanted to make that clear to all. Though such a basic reality should have been welcomed in a nation that pledged to follow the tradition of God and His Prophet, for some it just did not work with their personal plans.

Hence, they came to Ali on multiple occasions and in various iterations of advice, counsel, and recommendations to be more lenient in his implementation of social justice programs.

"Let some things slide," they suggested. "The people will grow tired of this," they warned. "Keep them close to you," they said.

Ali responded as he did many times before, "I do not double-deal in matters of my faith and I will not be compromised by the wretched." Ali's love for Islam was too great to be compromised. That true love made his commitment to the path of God unwavering.

Seeing the rigidness of his belief and the firmness of his principle, things got complicated, not just in Medina, but across the empire. Talhah, Zubayr, and Saad ibn Abi Waqqas withdrew their allegiance to Ali. A small group followed them in Medina. Muawiya and his stronghold in Damascus refused to pay allegiance to Ali. Abu Moussa Al-Ash'ari in Kufa held a spiteful position against the new caliphate.

The air filled with an irrational malevolence and viciousness toward the new caliphate. Still, some of the reasons can be identified as the reader takes a closer look into the individuals at play and their possible motives.

Aisha was notably in the ranks of the opposition that revolted against Uthman during his caliphate. She vehemently opposed his policies and decreed that he had strayed so far off the path of Islam that he should be killed. The opposition revolted against Uthman and his administration in an elaborate fashion.

They spread his weaknesses, tarnished his reputation, hurried to support any rebellions taking place around the empire, and exposed his nepotism and unjust favoritism to the tribes of Umayya and Abu Mu'eet.

History tells us that Uthman ascended the pulpit one afternoon at the Prophet's Mosque. As he was delivering his sermon to those present, Aisha entered the mosque. She walked in displaying the shirt of the Prophet. As she held it for the people to see she said,

"This is the robe of the Holy Prophet! It has not worn out yet, but Uthman has worn out his tradition."

Uthman's color changed and was visibly affected by her words. He lifted his hands to the sky and said, "Lord, relieve me from their schemes. Indeed, their schemes are grand..."

When Aisha saw that people were resolved on the killing of Uthman, she turned to him and said, "Indeed, Uthman. You made the treasury of the Muslims your own personal bank account. You let the sons of Umayya loose on the wealth of the Muslims, and appointed them as governors of the lands.

"You left the nation of Muhammad to hardship and distress. May God cut you off from His grace and blessing. May He deprive you from the bounties of the Earth. For if it were not for the fact that you pray the five, they would have slaughtered you like a camel…"

When Uthman was surrounded and the people's enmity and sensation of vengeance had reached its boiling point, Aisha made her infamous statement. "Kill Na'thal, for he has disbelieved." Aisha repeated this statement more than once. It was a message of validation to the rebels.

Her illustration of Uthman – especially from her status and position, which was bolstered during the first two caliphates – with the word "Na'thal" could have two meanings; both having a considerable effect on public opinion. One, the word literally means hyena. Two, it was the name of a Jewish man in Medina who was known for his enmity towards the faith. Consequently, the caliph was painted as both a lowly animal and an enemy of the faith.

As the situation increased in tension and Uthman's position weakened, Aisha announced that she was making her way to Mecca. She left the people to deal with Uthman as they pleased. The caliph felt the pressure of the position he was in. He sent

Marwan ibn Al-Hakam and Abd al-Rahman ibn 'Utab in an attempt to have her stay and postpone her trip to Mecca.

"I've started my journey and obliged myself with this pilgrimage, so by God I will not postpone…"

She then turned to Marwan and said, "O' Marwan, you seem to think that I am a suspect in the matter of your friend… By God, if I wanted him in one of my schemes, I would have run circles around his rule and thrown him to the sea."

People understood Aisha's departure from Medina as a symbolic declaration of war against Uthman, especially with her rejection of the caliphate's call to stay in Medina to help keep calm and de-escalate the plans of the rebels.

As Aisha finished the rituals of Hajj, she was informed of Uthman's murder. She hurried back to Medina as to ensure she would have a say in the appointment of the next caliph. On her way to Medina, Aisha crossed paths with a man leaving the city.

"What news comes from the city?" she asked the man approaching.

"Uthman has been killed," he replied.

"Damn the Hyena and thank God we are rid of him… What has transpired thereafter?"

"The people of Medina came together for a consensus on the next caliph, and they came to the best decision. They agreed on Ali ibn Abi Talib."

"By God, it would have been better if the skies crashed into this Earth! The matter is in his hand now?! Is what you're saying true?"

"It is as I said, O' Mother of the Believers," he replied.

Aisha turned red in the face and let out a series of moans and groans. She was beyond furious.

"What is wrong, O' Mother of the Believers? By God, I do not know anyone better than him, more deserving than him, or anyone who can compare to him in any shape or facet. So, what do you hate about him?"

"Uthman was killed unjustly and oppressed... I will avenge his blood."

"But you were the first to attack and denigrate him. You told the people, 'Kill the Hyena, for he has disbelieved.'"

"By God, I spoke, and the people spoke. But the last of my words will be better than the first..."

She returned to Mecca. The people were gathered around her at the Kaaba as she stood before the door of the House of God. They looked to her and she spoke,

"O' people, Uthman was killed unjustly and oppressed. By God, I will avenge his blood. O' people of Quraysh, Uthman has been murdered! Ali ibn Abi Talib killed him! By God, one day under Uthman is better than an entire decade with Ali."

Aisha launched her campaign openly against Ali. She did not hold back. Her campaign can be explained by two possibilities.

For one, Aisha had nothing but spite for Ali since day one. She envied him for the Prophet's unmatched love and care for Ali. She was bothered by the fact that the Prophet held Ali and Fatima, and their sons Hasan and Husayn, in a light that was special from the rest of the household.

After the Prophet passed, Aisha and Um Salama – both widows of the Prophet – were sitting together. Um Salama reminded Aisha of an incident that took place with the Prophet and Ali.

"Do you remember that day when Ali came to see the Prophet, and we were with him? Ali came down from his horse and greeted the Prophet. Together they walked away as the Prophet confided in Ali. They were gone for a while, and you could not bear it.

"You wanted to go after them. I told you not to, but you would not listen. So, you went after them and returned to me shortly after crying. I asked you what was wrong. You told me that you went after them and found them speaking to each other in private.

"You said that you snapped at Ali saying, 'I only have one day out of every nine days with the Prophet, can you not just leave us alone on my day, Ali?' You said that the Prophet became red in the face, turned to you and said, 'Go back! By God, no one from my family has spite for him, nor anyone from the people, except that they are outside of faith!' You came back in remorse and defeat..."

"Yes, I remember that."

Aisha was the wife of the Prophet, but she did not enjoy the status and adornment that these individuals had. Her envy, which turned to spite, ate away at her. That all started with Ali.

In the end, Ali was the Prophet's most beloved. Ali was to Muhammad as Aaron was to Moses. Ali put his life on the line for Muhammad since he was a child. Muhammad saw no one more dedicated, capable, and pious than Ali. When the Prophet and Ali were in each other's company, it was only them. Ali was the Prophet's shadow ever since he was a little boy.

Muhammad raised him, and so no love in the world was like the love he had for Ali. For that, Aisha despised him.

The second possibility is that Aisha's opposition to Uthman was intended to pave the path for her cousin, Talhah ibn Ubaydallah. She and her cousin were from the same tribe – Banu Tameem.

There was a telling conversation that took place between Aisha and Ibn Abbas during the journey back to Mecca from Medina, as Uthman was being encircled by the rebels. Aisha left Medina at such a sensitive time, even when Uthman requested that she stay.

Perhaps it was a directive by Talhah, who was one of the leaders of that revolution against Uthman and one who had called for his death.

Aisha crossed paths with Ibn Abbas on the way to Mecca.

"O' Ibn Abbas, beware, do not let off from this tyrant Uthman! The people have been blinded. They have ravaged the lands of the people... I see Talhah ibn Ubaydallah taking control of the state treasury and the keys to its chests. If he is given power, he will lead on the path of his cousin, Abu Bakr."

"If something bad happens to the man, the people will not be taking refuge in anyone but our man (Ali)," Ibn Abbas replied to Aisha.

"Let it go, I do not want to hear your conceitedness or your bickering," Aisha replied sharply.

Talhah and Zubayr joined her opposition, even though they had just paid allegiance to Ali. They took the death of Uthman, and made it the mascot of their campaign to take down the caliphate of Ali. It was as if Aisha forgot that she was the first to call for the death of Uthman.

Her words, "Kill the Hyena, for he has disbelieved," echoed across the four corners of the empire. It was these words that unsheathed the swords of the rebels, and validated the murder of the caliph.

Talhah was a vesting force for the rebels. They rallied around him and looked to him for empowerment. He was their voice and the formidable grip around their swords... those swords that would slay the caliph.

Zubayr's silence was just as powerful as Talhah's voice. Such silence was a sign of acceptance and contentment with their unretractable actions. History would tell that Talhah was unmatched in his fierce opposition towards Uthman.

When the revolution took its course and Uthman was barricaded in his home, Talhah insisted that nothing be allowed to reach Uthman, not even a sip of water. Ali sent a message to Talhah to stop such nonsense, to allow the man access to water, and at the very least not to kill him thirsty. Talhah refused.

Not seeing any sign of responsiveness from him or the people surrounding the house, Ali sent three jugs filled with water to Uthman. Just before they arrived at the house, Talhah got wind of it and stopped them immediately. He saw Ali nearby and exploded, furiously yelling in the face of Ali.

"What do you have with this?! Leave it be, O' Ali!"

But Ali could not just leave it be. They exchanged words and Talhah remained adamant on keeping the man thirsty. Moments later the men climbed into the house of Uthman, breaking in through the rooftops, and killed Uthman.

As the men left the house, they looked around asking, "Where is Talhah ibn Ubaydallah? We have killed Uthman ibn Affan..."

What is peculiar is the fact that those who wanted Uthman dead, and made sure that he was killed through their influence and prowess, were the same individuals who sought vengeance for his death. Aisha and Talhah facilitated the assassination of the caliph in directing the anger of the rebels toward the house of Uthman.

They assumed they would be able to bring the caliphate back to their tribe of Banu Tameem, with Talhah as the new caliph. But their plan quickly evaporated when the people gravitated to

Ali ibn Abi Talib as the only choice as caliph. It was only after that point, when Ali accepted the people's nomination, that Aisha and Talhah suddenly took up the campaign of vengeance for the blood of Uthman.

And who were they to take their vengeance from? Ali.

Their vengeance was not for the blood of Uthman, which they ultimately orchestrated. It was for Ali taking what they thought belonged to them – the helm, the throne, the caliphate. Both Talhah and Zubayr had paid allegiance to Ali, with the hopes that Ali would position them as governors over Iraq and Yemen. They made their political ambitions clear after they paid homage to the new caliphate, but Ali did not entertain their bargaining.

Talhah and Zubayr came to Ali's home one night to speak to him about their future role in the caliphate. Upon their entering, Ali blew out one candle on his desk and lit another candle next to it.

"Do you know why we have paid you allegiance?" Talhah hurriedly asked Ali without sitting down.

"Yes, on the basis of respect and obedience, and on the same basis you paid allegiance to Abu Bakr, Umar, and Uthman," Ali responded firmly.

"No, rather we have pledged allegiance to you on the basis that we are your partners in governance," Talhah responded.

Ali replied swiftly, "No. But you are partners in speaking with integrity and aiding in eradicating deficits and corruption."

After a moment of pause, Zubayr asked, "Why did you blow out one candle and light another when we first arrived?"

The first candle was purchased from the funds of the public treasury; I was busy with the affairs of the state, so I continued to use it. Since you have come here with a private matter, I decided to light this other candle, purchased from my own personal funds.

Talhah and Zubayr looked at one another blankly. The man would not even burn a candle outside of its purpose, so how could he appoint them to positions of power for merely paying homage? They left the house of Ali disappointed.

When their interests could not be realized through any other means, the three of them – Talhah, Zubayr, and Aisha – took to a campaign that would bring thousands of Muslims to the battlefield and challenge Ali's caliphate at its onset.

CHAPTER 18

THE BATTLE OF THE CAMEL

You will fight Ali and you will have oppressed him.

– Muhammad

Even though hostility and hatred existed amongst some, most of the nation was behind its leader – Ali. They found it intolerable that Ali was going to be accused, betrayed, and fought in such a way – especially as the new caliph who had just assumed his role. They begged him to lead them, and now others wanted to drag him down into their schemes. They would not allow it.

The new opposition against Ali gathered in the house of Aisha in Mecca. Talhah, Zubayr, Abdullah ibn Amer, and Ya'li ibn Manbeh ibn Umayya were present. They cried over the calamity of Uthman, shedding nothing but crocodile tears.

Yesterday they chanted, "Kill the Hyena, for he has disbelieved," and orchestrated his assassination, while today they cried over his bloodied body. Still, change can happen overnight, and it did.

"We must avenge him," they turned to one another with a vengeance that could only bring forth the bloodiest of wars. Their war would be against the caliph of their time – no easy feat.

But where would the blood be shed? Where could such a grand standoff take place? The widow of the Prophet and a band of his companions challenging his most beloved Ali, the Commander of the Faithful.

Mecca and Medina were not options, since the caliphate's capital was in Medina, and its influence extended well into Mecca. Basra and Kufa were suggested as options, as Talhah and Zubayr had men and influence in those cities.

Before the battle, as the people who followed Aisha and her companions rallied against Ali, he explained things beautifully:

> "They are demanding of me a right which they have abandoned, and a blood that they have themselves shed. If I were a partner with them in it, then they too have their share of it. But if they did it without me, they alone have to face the consequences. Their biggest argument against me is really against themselves.
>
> …They are suckling from a mother who is already dry, and bringing into life innovation that is already dead. How disappointing is this challenger to battle? Who is this challenger and for what is he being responded to? I am happy that the reasoning of God has been exhausted before them and He knows all about them."

The opposition chose Basra and marched on to southern Iraq. The defectors in Medina joined them and made their way to the city to take part in the battle against the new caliph, under the banner of Aisha, Talhah, and Zubayr. When Ali was informed of their campaign for war, he sent word to Aisha and the companions to reconsider their campaign for blood.

His message fell on deaf ears. They wanted nothing short of asserting their single aim to fight him and rid him of the caliphate. Their persistence was clear. They wanted war. What cemented this was their attack on Basra.

Talha and Zubayr launched an assault on the city of Basra. The raid took place in the middle of the night, catching its governor, Uthman ibn Hunayf, by surprise. They quelled their opposition quickly and killed dozens of men. Talha and Zubayr took over the headquarters of the Basra government and had its governor arrested and beaten.

With this audacious display of aggression, Ali prepared himself for an inevitable battle.

Before the battle, Aisha had a peculiar experience. On the road to Basra, she heard a group of dogs barking along the banks of a small body of water. She stopped in her tracks with a look of deep concern.

She turned to the men around her and asked, "Where are we? What waters are these?"

"Al-Haw'ab," they replied.

Aisha trembled.

"We are for God and to Him we shall return. I cannot stay here, I am leaving." Aisha turned her camel around.

"Wait! What's wrong? Why?" They responded.

Aisha replied nervously, "I heard the Prophet speak to his women one day and say, 'It is as if that I see the dogs of Al-Haw'ab bark at one of you... Beware that it is not you, O' Humayraa...'" Humayraa was a nickname of Aisha.

Muhammad ibn Talhah impatiently replied, "Come forward, may God have mercy on you. And do not trouble yourself with such words, we already passed Al-Haw'ab."

Abdullah ibn Zubayr swore to her by God that this was not Al-Haw'ab, that they had already passed it up. Muhammad ibn Talhah also fetched some locals to swear to her that this was not the Al-Haw'ab she spoke of. Reluctantly reassured, Aisha continued her path to Basra with thousands of men behind her to wage war on the Caliph of the Muslims.

It was as if they had forgotten the Prophet's words, "Whoever fights the Imam of their time will die as a disbeliever."

Aisha assembled her troops in Basra. Several distinguished men of opinion came to her and discussed the matter of war before Aisha. They tried to dissuade her from pursuing this battle and avoid bloodshed, suggesting that perhaps there were other means to achieve her goals. Their attempts were rendered futile, for she refused. Aisha was adamant in toppling Ali's caliphate that had just begun. At this point, Ali ibn Abi Talib had only been caliph for four months.

Abdullah ibn Abbas told of a small encounter he had with Ali prior to the Battle of the Camel. He said that when Ali set out for war with the people of Basra, he came to his audience at Dhi Qar and saw that Imam Ali was stitching his shoe.

Ali looked Abdullah and asked him, "What is the value of this shoe?"

Seeing that to the answer to the question was quite obvious, Abdullah answered simply, "It is of no value."

"By God, this shoe would have more value to me than the caliphate, but for the fact that I may establish right and ward off wrong through it."

Ali would then rise from his seat and go out to speak to the people:

Verily, God sent Muhammad when none among the Arabs read a book or claimed prophethood. He guided the people till he took them to their correct position and their salvation. So, their spears became straight and their conditions settled down.

By God, surely I was in their lead till it took shape with its walls. I did not show weakness or cowardice. My existing march is also like that. I shall certainly pierce the wrong till right comes out of its side.

What cause of conflict is there between me and the Quraysh? By God, I have fought them when they were unbelievers and I shall fight them when they have been misled. I shall be the same for them today as I was for them yesterday. By God, the Quraysh only take revenge against us because God has given us preference over them. So, we have allowed them into our domain, whereupon they have become as the former poet says:

By my life, you continued drinking fresh milk every morning,
And continued eating fine stoned dates with butter
We have given you the nobility which you did not possess
before
And protected you with thoroughbred horses and tawny-
colored spears...

The drums of war thundered in the land. The armies were
gathered in the battlefield. The open plains filled with an eerie
chill. But before the swords could speak, Ali came out into the
center of the battlefield, standing between the two armies. He
came out riding on the Prophet's mule, Al-Shuhbaa.

Ali was not holding any weapons; he rode without his sword
or spear. In that state, he was fully exposed, vulnerable to the
swords of his enemies. But he chose such vulnerability willingly,
something that most warriors would never in their wildest
dreams consider. Yet, this was a different kind of warrior.

This was Ali, the man with fear of nothing but the displeasure
of his Lord. Though Ali did not carry his sword, he was armed
with his unwavering belief and relentless justice.

Ali called Zubayr out into the open field.

Zubayr reluctantly complied and met him in the middle of
the battlefield.

"What made you come out here?" he asked Zubayr.

"The blood of Uthman," Zubayr replied in short.

"By God, I ask you Zubayr, do you not remember when you were walking with the Prophet as he came to me that one day… he was holding on to your arm, and as he greeted me, he gave me a great smile and laugh. He then turned to you and said, 'You will fight Ali and you will have oppressed him.'"

Shaken, Zubayr replied, "Yes, by God, I remember."

"Then on what basis are you fighting me?" Ali asked solemnly.

"By God, I forgot all about this. Had I remembered this, I would never have come out here, nor would I fight you, Ali," Zubayr lowered his head in regret and remorse.

Ali called unto Talhah, and then Aisha, and gave them similar reminders. They were not phased, and their position remained unchanged.

On the eve of the battle, Zubayr showed great hesitation. He was found speaking to himself and others about "this being the Sedition we have spoken of." Talhah was also scared, but he pulled himself together. He kept trying to convince himself that what he was doing was right, and it was in the end for the greater good.

Aisha was no different. It was a struggle within, no doubt, especially given the fact that they were some of the first to hear the Prophet say, "Ali is with the Truth, it turns wherever he may go."

They forced him to the battlefield and tomorrow they would be facing off with Truth. Were they fighting against the Truth? Did they wish the Truth to die?

The war drums thundered asunder and the hour of battle had begun.

The armies faced off once again and came in closer. Aisha's army was led by the tribe of Mudhar at the center, tribes from Yemen on the right flank, and the tribe of Rabee'a at the left flank. Their hearts were in their throats. Ali's army was led by his son, Muhammad ibn Al-Hanafiya, at the center, Ammar ibn Yasser on the right flank, and Aisha's brother, Muhammad ibn Abu Bakr, on the left flank. Their hearts were steady and their tongues sang the praises of God.

When the Commander of the Faithful gave his son, Muhammad ibn Al-Hanafiyya, the flag, he turned to him and said:

Mountains may move from their position, but you should not move from yours. Grit your teeth. Lend to God your head in fighting for Him. Give yourself to God. Plant your feet firmly on the ground. Have your eye on the remotest foe and close your eyes to their great numbers. Remember, your aid comes from God alone, the Glorified.

The time of battle had come. Ali looked to all his men and reminded them of their duty before God and the nation. He advised them of their state of mind during the fight:

The retreat after which return is intended, and the withdrawal after which attack is in view should not make you unhappy. Do justice to your swords. Keep ready a place for the falling of bodies of your foe; prepare yourselves for hurling strong spears and striking swords with full force and keep your voices down, as that keeps off cowardice.

By Him who broke open the seed for growing and created living beings, they had not accepted Islam, but they had secured safety by verbally professing it, and had hidden their misbelief. Consequently, when they found helpers for their misbelief, they disclosed it.

Swords sang, and their songs echoed in the battlefield for hours. Thousands of lives were taken. On that day, Talhah was also killed – but not by the forces of Ali. Talhah's killer was no other than Marwan ibn Al-Hakam, one of Uthman's men. He joined the ranks of Talhah in his campaign to avenge Uthman's blood, but he would do so in his own way.

During the battle, Talhah became preoccupied with the scene. Marwan stood at a distance and waited for the right moment. As Talhah grew deeper in his trance of the war that had ensued, Marwan drew his arrow and launched it, piercing Talhah and killing him.

"I do not demand vengeance for Uthman after this day!"

He pointed at the lifeless body of Talhah and continued, "The blood of Uthman was on his hands, as no one hated Uthman more than him."

After Zubayr spoke to Ali the day before, he went to Aisha and told her what was on his mind. He shared his hesitation and his reluctance to continue. He wanted nothing of this battle anymore.

"O' Abu Abdullah, are you frightened by the swords of the sons of Abd al-Muttalib?"

"Indeed, the swords of the sons of Abd al-Muttalib are long and sharp and held by young, honorable men!"

He turned to his son, Abdullah, and said, "You have your war; as for me, I am returning home."

"You're leaving now? When the matter is about to begin, and the parties have come to face one another? By God, we will not leave until it is finished!" Abdullah replied intensely.

"Do not mistake this for cowardliness on my part! I never fret from war, before Islam or after it," Zubayr insisted.

"Then what is making you retreat?"

"If you knew, it would break you," Zubayr replied to his son.

Abdullah ibn Zubayr took his father's role in leadership of the troops, while Zubayr returned home to Medina. But Zubayr never made it home: he was killed on his journey back to Medina.

Muhammad ibn Talhah and Abdullah ibn Zubayr led Aisha's troops into battle. The fighting was intense. The clashing of the swords continued for hours. At one point it seemed as if Ali's troops were losing advantage in the battle.

Where was Ali? He stood behind his troops looking on to the scores of men that had fallen. Ali lifted his hands to the Heavens and prayed to his Lord:

"My God, you know that I have not wronged Uthman with even a black mark on a white slate. But Zubayr and Talhah have gathered the people against me..."

Ali then stepped forth and plunged into the heart of the battle. The lion came out from its den, and no one could stand in its path. The battle continued and Ali's men gained the upper hand. Aisha sat on her camel in the midst of the battlefield, alone, with no one by her side. Abdullah ibn Zubayr was drenched in the blood of his wounds and Muhammad ibn Talhah was drowning in the heat of battle. Ali's warriors surrounded Aisha as her troops faced inevitable defeat.

The clangs of the swords came to a quiet, for the song had reached its end. Thousands of Muslims were killed. Aisha gazed upon the thousands of men that lay dead around her camel. One of Ali's warriors approached her and grabbed the reins of her camel to escort her off the battlefield.

Raising her voice in protest, she scorned Ali, "What kind of man orders that the widow of God's Prophet be escorted by strangers?!"

The warrior removed his helmet and unveiled himself to her.

"It is I, your brother, Muhammad," he told his elder sister.

Dumbfounded, Aisha was taken off the battlefield and escorted back to her home without scorn or harassment. Her camel was reigned in, and the battle was over. The battle would be named, "the Camel," after the camel of Aisha. With her camel came the battle, and with it the battle ended. And as she left, the corpses of thousands of fathers, husbands, and sons of the nation remained.

CHAPTER 19

A DAMNED GROUP

O' Muslims, I did not fight you so that you may pray, fast, and perform the pilgrimage. I have fought you only to rule over you.

– Muawiya ibn Abu Sufyan

Vengeance for Uthman's blood became the battle cry for anyone who wished to challenge Ali's caliphate. Just like Aisha, Talhah and Zubayr marched on to battle against Ali, Muawiya would do the same.

With this battle, the bodies of truth and falsehood could not be more distinct. On one side stood Ali, the brother and extension of the Holy Prophet. "Ali is from me, and I am from Ali," the Prophet would repeat to those near and far.

On the other side stood Muawiya, the son of Abu Sufyan and the chief of the Umayyads. Abu Sufyan was the Prophet's greatest enemy. Muawiya was raised in the house that cursed the Prophet's name, and swore vengeance against anything that lived and breathed in his praise.

"By the name that I swear by, there is no Heaven nor Hell," were the words of Abu Sufyan at the outset of Uthman's caliphate. Muawiya's words were even more frightening:

"O' Muslims, I did not fight you so that you may pray, fast, and perform the pilgrimage. I have fought you only to rule over you."

What was so peculiar about that time was the extent to which Muawiya had successfully manipulated the hearts and minds of his people in Syria. Employing a propaganda machine equipped with orators, poets, and pseudo-scholars, Muawiya not only tarnished Ali's name, he constructed a whole new person that carried that name in the eyes of the common Syrian.

"Ali's name shall be cursed in every Friday prayer," Muawiya mandated. Across Syria, mosque leaders on Muawiya's payroll began their Friday sermons by cursing Ali ibn Abi Talib! It became business as usual. This was coupled with poetry and false narrations shared across Syrian communities singing the praises of Muawiya and his father, Abu Sufyan, while denigrating the qualities of Ali and his father, Abu Talib.

Muawiya carried on the legacy of his father and established the dynasty of the Umayyads – one that would last for nearly a century. A family that hated the Prophet and his religion, unable to conquer him as enemies of the faith, would enter the religion and conquer from within to establish a dominion that would rule farther than the eye could see.

The son of Abu Sufyan would pick up where Aisha and her companions left off at the Battle of the Camel. Regardless of the outcome of the battle, Muawiya was going for the caliphate. His army was assembled and was ready for war even before the Battle of the Camel had commenced. If Aisha and Talhah were victorious, he would fight them. And if Ali was the victor, he would fight him. No one would be spared, and no mercy would be shown.

Muawiya embodied the characteristics of a man who could stand and challenge Ali. His cunningness, devious intelligence, apathy towards religion, and abundance of resources empowered him to launch a compelling campaign against the caliphate of Ali. He easily bribed and lured swaths of people to his side, in addition to capitalizing on the freshness of the recent battle that took so many lives from both sides of the conflict.

It was the year 657. The blood had not yet dried from the sands of Basra. Ali did not want another war, especially after thousands had been killed at the Battle of the Camel months earlier. Still, Ali remained ready for battle. He was ready for anything, to protect Islam and the Muslims. Ali tried to dissuade Muawiya from battle, as he had attempted with the companions in the previous battle. He regarded the blood of his brethren as sacred and did not hurry to sacrifice such blood unless it was of the very last resort, of their own prerogative, and in the way of God. In his final appeal to Muawiya, Ali spoke of history and the present. He reminded Muawiya who Ali ibn Abi Talib was:

> You have called for war. Put the people aside and come out and fight me. Let us excuse both armies from fighting. Let this show whose hearts and eyes are veiled. I am Abu Hasan, the killer of your grandfather, your uncle, and your brother on the Day of Badr.

The sword I used then is with me now. With that same heart
I stand before my enemies. I did not change my faith or my
prophet. I am on the same path that you left in obedience but
entered with spite...

Muawiya would never face Ali alone: he knew he stood no
chance in that on the battlefield. He would not risk his own life.
But that did not stop him from waging a war that would take the
lives of thousands of others.

The battle between the sons of Umayya and the sons of Abd
al-Muttalib would take place at Siffin. Muawiya rallied all the
men of Syria and marched on to the destination of battle. Ali departed Kufa with his army and they finally met the Syrians on
the plains of Siffin. Before settling into Siffin, for what would be
over a hundred days of encampment, Ali spoke to his army and
laid out his expectations of them:

Do not fight them unless they initiate the fighting, because,
by the grace of God, you are in the right and to leave them
till they begin fighting will be another point from your side
against them. If, by the will of God, the enemy is defeated,
then do not kill him who runs away, do not strike a helpless
person, and do not finish off the wounded.

Do not attack their women, even if they may attack your
honor with filthy words and abuse your officers... Be generous in your remembrance of God, so that you may be victorious.

In his outlining of the etiquettes of combat, he laid out the ethics of Islam. Ali distinguished himself as that immaculate leader with a divine purpose, teaching his soldiers that the meaning of life is not lost in war. Rather, if one engages in battle, it is only to defend the purpose for which he lives – to breathe the air of justice and have his heart beat to the rhythm of truth.

Ali did not fabricate this or put up a façade to falsely inspire his troops and boost their morale. You cannot make this up, it has to be a part of you. These words manifested the intellect and passion that was Ali ibn Abi Talib. As he would before any battle facing his enemy, Ali would invoke his Lord in supplication:

> O My Lord, hearts are drawn to You, necks stretch toward You, eyes are fixed on You, steps are in motion towards You and bodies have turned lean. My Lord, hidden animosity has become manifest and the cauldrons of malice are boiling. My Lord, we complain to You of the absence of our Prophet, the numerousness of our enemy and the diffusion of our passions. Our Lord, decide between us and between our people with truth, and You are the Best of Deciders.

Before the battle had commenced, and upon arrival to Siffin, Ali found that Muawiya's troops had taken control over the banks of the Euphrates river. The soldiers of Ali's camp were barred from access to water. Ali's scouts returned to him and let him know of this crucial matter. Without access to the primary water source in that region, they could not survive. Ali sent one of his men, Sasaah ibn Suhan, a companion of the Prophet, to Muawiya to ask for free access to the water for all sides. Muawiya refused. He saw an opportunity for Ali's army to be defeated by thirst, even before the battle had begun. He was going to seize that opportunity.

Sasaah returned with the news of Muawiya's refusal. A day passed and nightfall came. The men suffered. Their bodies grew weak in the unforgiving heat of Siffin. Dehydration especially took a toll on the elderly sergeants of the army, many of whom were companions of the Prophet Muhammad. In Ali's army at Siffin, there were 70 veterans from the Battle of Badr and 250 companions of the Prophet. Ali could not bear to see his men in such a condition. He called Malik al-Ashtar, one of his commanders and closest companions. Malik was a brave warrior, known across Arabia for his valor. He was also a loyal follower of Ali. His admiration for the man was almost unmatched by his contemporaries. Some say that Ali said, "Malik is to me as I was to the Messenger of God."

Ali ordered Malik al-Ashtar to take control of the waterfront at once. Malik's battalion was a force to be reckoned with. Soon enough, the battalion took over the riverfront and controlled access to the water source. The tables had turned and Muawiya's army came requesting access to the water.

Muawiya asked his advisor, Amr ibn al-Aas, worriedly, "Do you think Ali will deny us like we denied him?"

"Ali does not do what you do. He has a different purpose here," Amr replied, reassuring his comrade.

Triumphant, some of Ali's soldiers wanted to deny them just as they had been denied earlier. Ali would not have it. He opened the water to anyone who wished to drink, regardless of whether they were Muawiya's rebels or not. He said:

> The river belongs to God. There is no embargo on water for anyone, and whoever wishes, may take it from it.

That instant alone had a tremendous impact on some of the soldiers at Siffin. Many of the Syrians had not dealt with Ali. They only knew of him from the pulpits of the pseudo-scholars that cursed his name. The fact that Ali allowed them water, while their leader Muawiya would deny him, spoke volumes of the character of Ali. The following night, a group of Muawiya's rebels defected from his army and joined the ranks of Ali. Nevertheless, the battle would begin.

Three days of intense battle ensued and in those days the Angel of Death reaped many souls. Rivers of blood flowed from debauched limbs. Darkness cast over the battlefield and gloomed over the men, living and dead. The days were unforgiving and the nights sorrowful.

The Umayyad army had gained an upper hand at one point and Ali spoke to his men candidly. During the battle, he turned to his soldiers:

> I am faced with men who do not obey when I order, and do not respond when I call them… What are you waiting for to rise for the cause of God? Does not faith join you together, or a sense of shame rouse you? I stand among you shouting, and I am calling you for help, but you do not listen to my

word, and do not obey my orders, till circumstances bear out their bad consequences.

No blood can be avenged through you and no purpose can be achieved with you. I called you for help of your brethren, but you made noises like the camel having pain in its stomach, and became loose like the camel of thin back. Then a wavering, weak contingent came to me from amongst you: 'as if they are being led to death and they are only watching.'
– Holy Quran 8:6

Ali would come out into the middle of the battlefield, as the swords clanged and sung melodies of a confused heroism. He saw Muawiya in the distance, watching the battle, gazing over the thousands of men fighting for his greed. The lion roared and called out the fox.

For what reason do these men kill and be killed? Come out and fight me, Muawiya, and let the men be. Rule will be for the victor.

The challenge was clear and quite reasonable. But then again, who is the challenge initiated by, and who is being challenged here? The challenger is Ali, who holds Dhulfiqar, the sword gifted to the Prophet, and on to Ali from God's angels. The challenged is Muawiya, a politician and not a warrior.

Muawiya looked around at his company. He found their eyes glued to the valiant knight who challenged them. Their eyes were locked on the source of fear that entered their hearts. Their feet stopped in their tracks. They could not move. Muawiya snapped them back into reality, asking them their opinion in the matter.

Amr ibn Al-Aas replied mockingly, "The man picked you, go out and accept his challenge."

"You seem eager in the matter Amr… has Ali faced off with anyone and not killed him?" Muawiya replied back smugly.

"Are you too cowardly in the face of Ali that you try to flip my words on me? I will go out there and fight him myself!" Amr responded to Muawiya hastily.

Amr grabbed his sword and shield and headed for the battle-field. The men were in disbelief. Amr was in disbelief. He knew he could not fight Ali, but he said he would, and he could not walk back now. His honor was at stake, and if he retreated, he would be the laughing stock of the army.

Amr came before the grandeur of Ali and gazed at him for a while. He stood in awe. Amr was quickly reminded of his purpose in entering the battlefield and made the first strike against the Lion of God.

Within moments, Ali overpowered him and struck the sword and shield out of Amr's hands. Amr faced imminent death as his eyes watched the sword of Ali, Dhulfiqar, raised above him. To escape mortality, Amr did the unspeakable. He shed his clothes and exposed himself, right as Ali's sword was about to slice him in two.

The lewdness of Amr interrupted Ali's thunderous strike as he turned away from the indecent exposure. Amr escaped from Ali's hands and ran back to the tents of his camp disgraced.

In the battle that ensued, one of the earliest and most senior companions of the Prophet Muhammad would be martyred – Ammar ibn Yasir. As a commander in Ali's army, his old age of nearly eighty-seven did not hinder his valor and courage. He was eager to meet a fate that the Prophet had promised him. "O' Ammar, the transgressors will kill you…"

Ammar was killed on the battlefield of Siffin by Muawiya's men. Though it was a heartbreaking moment for the lovers of Muhammad and Ali, the promise of the Prophet was indeed fulfilled. The Prophet's promise to Ammar was known to many. His saying, "Ammar will be killed by the transgressors," was echoed in the battlefield. The side of truth could not be clearer. Though twenty-five years had passed since his own death, the Prophet had given his decree on that day. Ammar was guaranteed paradise by the Prophet, while Ammar's killers were designated as oppressors and transgressors. But did Muawiya and his men heed or reflect on the Prophet's words? They had other interests in mind.

Ali's army gained the upper hand, and it was as if the battle was decided. Fabricating a sense of calm and collection, Muawiya turned to Amr and asked him,

"So, what do you think we should do, Abu Muhammad? Have you not asserted that whatever bind you face, you have a way to escape from it?"

"War plays the odds. One day it's for us, another day it's upon us," Amr responded coldly.

Muawiya continued to remain calm, knowing that Amr wished to prove himself to Muawiya. After all, Muawiya had yet to give him his full share of Egypt's treasury as well as its full authority in governance.

"O' Amr, the night of Ali's victory is upon us... so what do you make of this?"

> Your men cannot beat his men, and you are not like him. He fights you for a purpose and you fight him for something else. You want to live a long life, and he wants to die with his honor. The people of Iraq fear you if you were to be victorious, but the people of Syria do not fear Ali... Give them a matter in which, if they accept it, there shall be discord, and if they reject it, there shall also be discord. Call them to take the Book of God as a judge between you... an arbitration – that will resolve your matter.

Muawiya nodded his head, impressed with Amr's cunning recommendation. "You tell the truth," Muawiya said to his friend. Tomorrow would see the conspiracy of *Tahkeem* – the Arbitration.

CHAPTER 20

THE BEGINNING OF A CONSPIRACY

Yesterday, I was the Commander of the Faithful, but today I am being commanded... You wish to be let to live, and I cannot coerce you for something you detest.

– Ali

The blistering morning would come to greet both armies, preparing them for battle.

Yet, the Syrians did not move from their place. They did not advance into the battlefield. Instead, a man from their army walked alone towards the army of Ali, raising the Book of God in his one hand.

"God, O' God, in the matter of our blood and your blood... between us is the Book of God!"

Other men behind him followed suit, placing copies of the Quran on their spears and chanting with the same call.

And there was the beginning of it all... the tides turned at that very moment and Muawiya saw victory through that simple gesture.

The night before, Al-Ash'ath ibn Qays spoke to his companions in the camp of Ali about their situation:

"O company of Muslims! You have seen what happened in the day which has passed. In it some of the Arabs have been annihilated. By God, I have reached the age which God willed that I reach. But I have never ever seen a day like this. Let the present convey to the absent!

If we fight tomorrow, it will be the annihilation of the Arabs and the loss of what is sacred. I do not make this statement out of fear of death, but I am an aged man who fears for the women and children tomorrow if we are annihilated. O God, I have looked to my people and the people of my deen and not empowered anyone.

There is no success except by God. On Him I rely and to Him I return. Opinion can be both right and wrong. When God decides a matter, He carries it out, whether His servants like it or not. I say this and I ask God's forgiveness for me and you."

On that very same night, Muawiya spoke to his men with words that were oh too similar:

"If we meet tomorrow the Byzantines will attack our women and children, and the people of Persia will attack the women and children of Iraq. Those with forbearance and intelligence see this. Tie the copies of the Quran to the ends of the spears."

Was it merely a coincidence that such a narrative was pushed within both camps right after the recommendation of Amr to Muawiya? And the very next day, it manifested itself so perfectly. Muawiya and Amr's plan married perfectly with the words of Al-

Ash'ath to the men in Ali's camp. So much so that some of the men in Ali's army sympathized with those who came out with the revelation on their spears.

Al-Ash'ath was swayed by the secret messengers of Muawiya, amongst them being Muawiya's brother, 'Uqba ibn Abu Sufyan. In the end, Al-Ash'ath admitted that his loyalty to Ali was only for protection and cover. It was a matter of interest and self-preservation. Others in Ali's company, like Amr ibn Al-Hamaq, saw things differently:

"O' Commander of the Faithful, we have not answered you and supported you out of fanaticism. We have answered your call only for God and we do not demand anything but justice," Amr ibn Al-Hamaq would say to Ali.

He, like Malik Al-Ashtar, Ammar ibn Yasser, and Hashim ibn 'Utba, did not see the camp of Ali as political cover and a means of survival in those turbulent times. They saw it as their moral duty, religious obligation, and holy call to answer and defend the faith against disunity, injustice, and oppression.

Still, the ranks were divided in the army of Ali as the whispers of Ibn Al-Aas and Al-Ash'ath filled their ears. Some of the men accepted nothing but war, while others saw that arbitration was the answer and not battle. Al-Ash'ath would take to the center of the scores of men who gathered before Ali, as he was red in the face and sweating from his brow.

O' Commander of the Faithful, we are with you today as we were with you before. But our situation recently is not as it used to be. None of the people is more loving to the people of Iraq and more loathing to the people of Syria than I am. So, answer these people to the Book of God, for you are more deserving to it than they are. The people hate to continue this fight… they want to live.

The matter became clearer at that moment, as Al-Ash'ath pressured further to accept the arbitration Muawiya's army so ardently pushed for. He was not leading this effort, Al-Ash'ath was being led.

At this point, no matter what Ali did in trying to show the truth in the matter before them, it fell on deaf ears and was presented to eyes that could not see. Ali saw how this would unfold. It was the scheming of Muawiya and he knew it oh too well. He raised his hands to the Heavens and prayed:

"My Lord, you know it is not the Book that they want. Be the judge between us, for you are the clear and evident Truth."

Malik Al-Ashtar, one of Ali's closest companions and commanders, had reached Muawiya's army and was about to launch an attack that would render the Syrians definite military defeat, and perhaps the death of Muawiya himself. He was so close he could taste victory. But just before Malik was about to attack, he received a message from Ali to turn back. With the furious insistence of Al-Ash'ath, and his band of men rallying for Ali to stop the war and accept arbitration, Ali called Malik back for his safety more than anything else. He feared that thousands of Al-Ash'ath's men were on the brink of mutiny, and if not dealt with delicately, they could turn on him and kill Malik.

When the messenger came to Malik and told him of Ali's order, Malik was taken aback.

"Do you not see that victory is near? Do you not see what God has given us? How can we leave now?!"

The messenger replied to Malik, "Do you wish to have victory here, while the Commander of the Faithful is offered to his enemies where he stands?"

Malik realized what was going on.

"By God, I could not bear that."

The messenger added, "They said and swore by him, 'Either you send Al-Ashtar back here, or we will kill you ourselves with our swords just as we killed Uthman. That or we will hand you over to Muawiya...'" describing the intensity of the situation within the ranks of Ali's army.

Malik nodded and immediately turned his unit around, back to the aid of Ali. Though military victory could have been met in those moments, it meant nothing if his leader was to be ambushed and sacrificed to the wolves.

The tides were turning in Muawiya's favor far too quickly, but it was a reality Ali had to face and deal with. He gathered his companions and spoke to them from his heart. He told his men that this heart of his had not changed, but that their fate would be dictated by these unholy circumstances.

"Yesterday, I was the Commander of the Faithful, but today I am being commanded... You wish to be let to live, and I cannot coerce you for something you detest."

After this, Al-Ash'ath would come back to Ali and make a recommendation:

"O' Commander of the Faithful, I see that the people are content and happy with the response to the other side in the invitation for arbitration by the Book of God. If you wish, I can go to Muawiya and see what he wants…"

The proposal was not much of a recommendation, as Ali knew Al-Ash'ath already had opened channels of communication with Muawiya and his brother. It was clear after the threats from Al-Ash'ath and his men that the swords that descended upon Uthman would likewise fall on him if he did not choose the path of arbitration and end the war.

Ali gave Al-Ash'ath permission to go and speak to Muawiya. Al-Ash'ath did not need the permission so much as he wanted to stamp a public perception that arbitration was being assented to from all sides.

Al-Ash'ath entered the camp of Muawiya and was greeted with open arms.

"Why did you use the copies of the Quran on spears?" Al-Ash'ath was boggled by the gesture.

"So that we may all return to what God commanded us with. Let us select a man from amongst us, and a man from amongst yourselves to be arbiters in the way of God's Book. Whatever they decide, we will follow…"

Enchanted by Muawiya's reason, "This is the truth," Al-Ash'ath replied to Muawiya.

When he returned to his camp, Al-Ash'ath told Ali of their conversation and the decision of arbitration in such a manner described.

Ali remained silent and looked off into the abode that once was filled with his warriors, but now looked only of miserly sheep.

CHAPTER 21

THEY WANTED ARBITRATION

His mandate is for us to clash our swords, just as he and you wanted...

– Abu Moussa Al-Ash'ari

Ibn Al-Aas and his ally Al-Ash'ath completed half of the task. The other half was to pick the right men for the arbitration to realize Muawiya's plan to its fullest.

The Syrians would choose Ibn Al-Aas as their arbiter and the ultimate representative of their side of the conflict. In the end, he was the fountainhead of this sedition, and the author of this entire scheme. Muawiya would not accept anyone other than him to assume this position anyway. Choosing Amr as their man was quick and decisive.

Ali's army, however, had much more difficulty in having a united front for choosing their own arbiter. Ali and his closest companions were resolute on having Abdullah ibn Abbas be their representative.

Al-Ash'ath was quick to oppose the nomination.

"We choose Abu Moussa Al-Ash'ari and we will not be content with anyone other than him!"

Ali quickly responded and made it known that Al-Ash'ari was not an acceptable choice to him. But Al-Ash'ath and his men did not care, and their responses grew only bolder.

"By God, we do not care, whether it's you or Ibn Abbas. We want a man from you and a man from Muawiya that can face each other equally, and not that either one is less than the other."

Ali then gave another suggestion. Malik Al-Ashtar.

Al-Ash'ath leaped in protest. "Is there not anyone on the face of this Earth for us but Al-Ashtar? Are we compelled to take the mandate of Al-Ashtar?"

"And what is his mandate?" Ali replied.

"His mandate is for us to clash our swords, just as he and you wanted…"

The camp was overcome by a deep silence.

Ali knew Al-Ash'ari too well. Al-Ash'ari was not qualified for such a crucial task. He was an old, weak man, whose heart and faith were more frail than his aging body. Months earlier, he had deserted Ali at the Battle of the Camel. In fact, he lobbied people away from joining Ali's ranks, did not participate in the battle himself, and was not found in the public eye until a month after the battle ended. Ali could not trust that such a man would be able to act justly when the stakes were so high.

Still, Al-Ash'ath and his men were adamant that Al-Ash'ari be their representative in the arbitration. They were a volatile bunch; though they called for arbitration and peace, they were willing to use their swords against their own commander.

"The people of Syria will not accept Ibn Abbas as an arbiter, because he's your relative and biased towards your cause," Al-Ash'ath explained to Ali. Of course, Ibn Abbas would not be accepted by Muawiya and Ibn Al-Aas, because he was a man of integrity and faith. He could not be swayed like the others.

The more Al-Ash'ath shouted, the more men joined him in their naïve nomination of Abu Moussa Al-Ash'ari. Ali looked at his soldiers, who stood before him with an uncanny stubbornness for Al-Ash'ath's position. They were opinionated. Ali did not mind having his men voice their opinions. He was used to engaging in dialogue and speaking to people with logic and reason. But logic and reason did not work. Their mulishness was alarming, and the matter was clear.

Ali calmed his men down and stood at the center of them.

"Have you refused everyone but Abu Moussa?"

He looked around and gazed into their eyes. He had his answer before they spoke.

"Yes!" They replied in unison.

"Then do as you wish."

This was not Al-Ash'ath's first overreaching interaction with Ali. Back in Kufa, the Commander of the Faithful was delivering a lecture from the pulpit when Al-Ash'ath interrupted in objection and said, "O' Commander of the Faithful, this thing is not in your favor but against you!"

Ali responded to him with an evident display of anger and disapproval.

"How do you know what is for me and what is against me? May God's damnation fall upon you. You are a weaver and son of a weaver. You are the son of an unbeliever and yourself a hypocrite. You were arrested once by the unbelievers, and once by the Muslims, but your wealth and birth could not save you from either. The man who contrives for his own people to be put to sword and invites death and destruction for them does deserve that the near ones should hate him and the remote ones should not trust him."

Since the day he took any position of leadership, Ali would not force his will upon people. He did not believe in coercing people or deceiving them into the fold of his plans or interests. That was not his style of leadership, nor did it fall within his ambition to establish the standard of just governance.

Several companions of Ali tried to dissuade Al-Ash'ath and his group from their nomination of Al-Ash'ari. He could not stand up to the trickery and cunningness of Ibn Al-Aas. Al-Ash'ath was an ally of Al-Aas, so it did not mean anything to his disadvantage.

Ali was resolute in not having his army split up into factions, and in keeping it as united as possible. For that reason, he acquiesced and told them to do as they pleased. For if he were to be heavy-handed and force his way, they would dismantle the army from within and Muawiya would have his sure victory. Still, Ali was not bashful in speaking his mind and telling the soldiers things as they truly were:

"O' those whose bodies are present, but their minds are absent. Those whose whims are various and their leaders are tribulated with them. Your leader obeys God, but you disobey him, yet the leader of Syria disobeys God, but his men obey him. I wish that Muawiya would give me the exchange of Dinar to Dirham, in that he takes ten of my men and gives me one of his…"

Al-Ash'ari was their choice and he went forward as the arbiter with Ibn Al-Aas from the opposing side. The two met at Dawmet Al-Jundul. Eyes from both camps could not see anything else but these two men. With their eyes, their hearts fixated on the fate that two men would decide. What would be the outcome of their deliberations? Could Abu Moussa withstand the cunning of Ibn Al-Aas? Only time would tell, and time here was only hours and minutes.

Before the meeting, many distinguished men within the camp of Ali came to speak to Al-Ash'ari, both to warn him of the cunningness of Ibn Al-Aas, and to advise him on the groups' best interests. Shureyh ibn Hani would sit with Al-Ash'ari and speak to him frankly:

"O' Abu Moussa, you have been appointed for a greatly important matter… Know that the people of Iraq will not survive under the rule of Muawiya, while the people of Syria would not have trouble under the reign of Ali. Keep this in mind…"

Al-Ahnaf ibn Qays warned him of the sensitivity of this whole ordeal:

"If you lose Iraq in this, there will be no Iraq for you… Fear God so that you may have both this world and the next. When you meet Amr tomorrow, do not offer him peace, because he is not of its people. Do not give him your hand, because it is a trust…"

Al-Ash'ari heard these warnings and much more from others in his midst.

Ibn Al-Aas was also given advice before the arbitration. Muawiya spoke to his man in confidence:

"O' Amr, the people of Iraq forced Ali's hand with the selection of Abu Moussa. The people of Syria and I, however, are happy with you as our selection. I hope that we can evade this war with the virtue of the Syrians' strength, Iraq's disunity, and the aid of Yemen… The man who has joined you has a big mouth but little in opinion."

In short, Amr and Al-Ash'ari were meeting for lunch, yet little did Al-Ash'ari know that he was lunch.

Al-Ash'ari had no opinion in the deliberation. It was merely Ibn Al-Aas telling him what should be done. Acting as if he was processing and contemplating the options, the weak and cowardly Al-Ash'ari did not take long to concede to Amr's proposal. The decision was to disavow both Ali and Muawiya in the matter of rulership, and instead have the people elect amongst themselves who they believed to be best to lead the nation. Amr and Abu Moussa agreed that they each make mirroring statements to show the unity in their decision as the conclusion of the arbitration. That was that. They ended their deliberation session and informed the armies they had come to a decision.

The armies gathered for the announcement. The companions of Ali stood by with hearts filled with genuine fear and concern over the fate of the nation. It rested upon the shoulders of Al-Ash'ari, who was weak in faith and feeble in character. His speech sang of loyalty, but his heart was the farthest from it.

The hearts of Muawiya's companions danced ecstatically with the outcome they were certain of. Their man was cunning and astute, a slithering, sly creature that could get his way, and bring his people what they wanted. He worked for his self-interest before anyone else, and that was the guarantee that he would get what he wanted.

Abu Moussa and Amr stood before the armies that gathered before them. Abu Moussa took a step forward and declared to the people, "I bear witness to what Amr will say." He turned to Amr and said, "Rise and tell the people what our opinions have come together on and what we agreed to."

"Glory be to God! How could I rise before you? God brought you into Islam and through the migration before me. You were the ambassador of the people of Yemen to the Messenger of God, and the Messenger's ambassador back to them. You rise before me please, and I will speak after you…"

Pleased with the superficial praise and words of admiration he received from his colleague, Al-Ash'ari complied with Amr's sentiment. Before he began speaking, Abdullah ibn Abbas called out to Al-Ash'ari.

"Abu Moussa! Beware! By God, he is tricking you. If you agreed to something, let him speak before you and then go ahead thereafter. Indeed, he is a backstabber…"

The vain and naïve Abu Moussa insisted otherwise. He fell into the trap, even when it stared him in the face. Perhaps, it was not a trap and rather he willingly took part in the scheme alongside Al-Ash'ath from the outset?

Abu Moussa stood to address the people with his statement of arbitration. He cleared his throat as Ibn Al-Aas stared at him with sharp focus.

"This sedition has eaten away at the Arabs… It is of my opinion and the opinion of my colleague, Amr, that both Ali and Muawiya are stripped from the matter of rulership. Let this matter be decided by council between the Muslims themselves, and they will choose whoever they deem fit to rule over them.

"I have disavowed both Ali and Muawiya in this matter, so take this matter and decide who you believe is best fit to lead."

Abu Moussa sighed and took a seat. Amr wore a great big smile and stood to address the people.

"You heard what he said. He disavowed his leader. I disavow his leader just as he did. And I assert my leader, Muawiya, for this matter, for he is the successor of Uthman, the avenger of his blood, and the most deserving of people for his position."

Amr then took a seat, laughing at all those he fooled. Abu Moussa, stunned, looked at him with eyes wide.

"What is wrong with you? Damn you! You stabbed me in the back and turned on me. You're like a dog, whether you're with it or you leave it, it will not stop panting…" Abu Moussa scorned Amr.

Amr with his smug smile replied, "And you're like a donkey that carries weight…"

Muawiya's plan worked. He used the arbitration not to strike peace and avoid military defeat. He used it to give his army the upper hand by creating discord and chaos in Ali's ranks. The arbitration solidified that and weakened the Alid caliphate only further.

Ali's men urged him to relaunch the war and once again engage in battle. He refused. The people asked for a ceasefire, and they got it. He was not going to change that now because they did not have the foresight to see the possible consequences that would not work in their favor. Ali was a man of his word, to his friends and foes alike.

Ali emphasized that his position would not change until the armistice ended. The conflict would not end with Muawiya: it was the eternal conflict between truth and falsehood.

After this disaster, a new plague was born in Islam. Out of Ali's army came a group called the Khawarij. They turned from soldiers who fought for Ali to swords raised against Ali and those with him. From there, they became a force that fought anyone who disagreed with them and who did not accept their version of Islam.

CHAPTER 22

THE KHAWARIJ

He is the Commander of the Faithful and the first Muslim who believed in God.

– Abdullah ibn Khabab

The days passed and the nation had yet to wipe the dirt from its brow after the calamities they faced in Siffin. Muawiya continued to scheme for his ultimate goal of reigning over the entire Muslim empire. But most of all, he wanted to be rid of Ali's caliphate. Everyone and everything was a tool in his hands to reach his objectives. Quagmires were turned into opportunities, and ardent foes could be made into loyal subjects. It just required the poetic rhetoric, a façade of piety, and most of all, money – all of which Muawiya had plenty of.

After Siffin and the resulting arbitration, which came to be known as Al-Tahkeem, an intriguing thing happened. Al-Ash'ath rallied thousands of men within the army to take the route of arbitration and stop the war. They accepted the gesture of the Quran on spears, which Ali warned his men was a trick of Muawiya. They pushed for arbitration, and threatened Ali if he would not assent to their desire. Those same men, whether they were loyal partners to Al-Ash'ath or were fooled and taken advantage of by him, would become the Khawarij.

They raged in a fury that was not even seen on the battlefield. They wanted to fight Muawiya and have his head in battle. Ali refused.

"I gave you that option yesterday, and when you chose an arbiter, I told you not to send Abu Moussa. But you did not obey me. There is no path to fight them, until the truce ends!" Ali made it clear.

The truce that took place as part of the decision to arbitrate, and end the battle, had four provisions. One, both armies would lay down their arms and neither side should engage the other for the entirety of the year. Two, the arbiters were obliged to provide a final ruling to their arbitration within this time period. Three, the people of Iraq were to return to Iraq and the people of Syria to return to Syria. Four, both sides would abide by this agreement during this time period.

The truce was promised for a year with its conditions. No matter what, Ali refused to break an agreement he entered. That was one of the virtues that distinguished him from the likes of Muawiya.

When the news had reached the ranks of Ali's soldiers, groups of them were in disbelief. They shouted furiously, "We made a mistake in accepting the arbitration and we will amend that mistake. Arbitration belongs to God alone!" That was the war cry of the Khawarij.

Truly, the Khawarij were an interesting bunch. Extremists in the plainest sense of the word, they built a culture of rushing towards death – both throwing themselves into it and dragging their enemies to it. The majority of them belonged to a group at that time known as the Qurra', who took to a very literal reading of the Holy Quran, and defended their beliefs militantly. Their extremism was what made them so irreligious and immoral.

To illustrate this point, one day, Abdullah ibn Khabab ibn Al-Arat was walking a certain road with his pregnant wife. A group of Khawarij stopped them and surrounded Abdullah and his wife in an interrogative manner. They asked him for his name. Abdullah replied that he was merely a believing man.

"What do you say about Ali ibn Abi Talib," they asked him.

"He is the Commander of the Faithful and the first Muslim who believed in God," Abdullah plainly replied.

"So, what is your name?"

"Abdullah ibn Khabab ibn Al-Arat, a companion of the Holy Prophet," he said.

"Did we scare you?" they replied in question.

"Yes," Abdullah said.

"Do not be scared! Tell us about your father, particularly about the words he heard from the Messenger of God. Perhaps God will benefit us with it."

"Sure," Abdullah responded nervously.

"My father told me that the Messenger of God said, 'There will be sedition after me, whereby the heart of a man will die just like his body dies, he will go to sleep as a believer but awake as an apostate.'"

Their circle closed in even tighter around Abdullah and his wife.

"It is this narration that we asked you for…" one of the men said as they grabbed Abdullah and his wife.

"By God, we will kill you in a way that we've never killed anyone!" the men threatened.

They took Abdullah and his wife and tied them by the hands. Abdullah's wife was at full term, ready to give birth any day. The men then found a date tree to sit underneath for its shade from the scorching sun. Some dates had fallen to the ground where they rested their feet. Some of the men picked up the dates and ate them.

As they chewed on the ripened dates, another amongst them scolded them, "You ate something that was not for you…"

One of the men went on to kill a wild hog that he saw, which was apparently owned by a Christian man living nearby. His companion reprimanded him as well.

"This is an act of corruption on God's Earth. Go, appease the man for killing his pig…"

When Abdullah ibn Khabab saw these acts, he pleaded to them.

"If you are truthful in what I see, then I should not have any misfortune with you. By God, I know nothing happens in vain in Islam. I am a believer, and you told me that I was safe and I had nothing to fear!"

They did not respond to Abdullah.

They took him and his wife next to the pig that was slaughtered by the river. Like the pig, they slaughtered Abdullah and saw his blood flow into the river. They then turned to his wife, who pleaded in agony of what she just witnessed.

"Please! I am just a woman. Do you not fear God?!"

They stabbed her in the abdomen and removed her baby out of her womb. As they watched her blood and organs flow out of her, they proceeded to behead her. They threw her body next to her husband's on the banks of the river.

These men scolded each other and felt shameful for eating fallen dates, but did not bat an eyelid at slaughtering a man, his wife, and their unborn child, like wild hogs.

The Khawarij went on to cause havoc in the nation, killing, crucifying and pillaging villages in the name of Islam. Ali would not tolerate such savagery. He would put a stop to it at once.

CHAPTER 23

THE BLOOD WOULD FLOW

The verdict is for God alone…

– The Khawarij

The murder of Abdullah ibn Khabab caused an uproar in the nation. The Muslims were enraged by such barbarism. The Khawarij prepared themselves for battle. They wanted rage. They wanted war. They wanted blood.

With the Khawarij threatening war and havoc, Muawiya did not remain in Syria to keep the peace. He took full advantage of the situation after the Battle of Siffin. Muawiya launched attacks on cities within the dominion of the Alid caliphate in Iraq. He sent thousands of troops to attack the Iraqi cities of Al-Mada'in (central Iraq), Al-Anbar (western Iraq), and Het (also near Al-Anbar). Al-Mada'in was deserted by its people, so Muawiya's commander, Sufyan ibn Awf Al-Ghamidi, went on to Anbar. Only five hundred soldiers loyal to the caliphate were stationed in the city. Of those five hundred, only a hundred remained firm to their positions. They fought valiantly against the force of five thousand Umayyads. The leader of the one hundred was Hasan ibn Hasan Al-Bakri. He was killed with his men. Anbar was ransacked and the city was leveled to the ground.

Upon hearing the news, Ali ascended the pulpit and pressed the men of the mosque to join the ranks of the army and fight against these invaders. They remained, and no one answered his call from those present. They did not have the appetite for battle. Disgusted by their apathy, he left the pulpit to face the enemy himself on foot. Moved and feeling a sense of guilt, they followed him. A force of eight thousand soldiers was mobilized, but by the time they moved to face Sufyan ibn Awf, it was too late. The force of eight thousand returned without engagement.

Ali was devastated. He went back to the pulpit and delivered the following sermon:

> Surely jihad is one of the doors of Paradise, which God has opened for His chief friends. It is the dress of piety and the protective armor of God and His trustworthy shield. Whoever abandons it, God covers with the dress of disgrace and the clothes of distress. He is kicked with contempt and scorn, and his heart is veiled with screens of neglect. Truth is taken away from him because of missing jihad. He has to suffer ignominy and justice is denied to him.

> Beware! I called you to fight these people night and day, secretly and openly and exhorted you to attack them before they attacked you, because, by God, no people have been attacked in the hearts of their houses, but they suffered disgrace; but you put it off to others and forsook it, till destruction befell you and your cities were occupied. The horsemen of Banu Ghamid have reached al-Anbar and killed Hasan ibn Hasan al-Bakri. They have removed your men from the garrison.

I have come to know that every one of them entered upon Muslim women and other women under protection of Islam and took away their ornaments from legs, arms, necks and ears and no woman could resist it, except by pronouncing the verse,

"We are for God and to Him we shall return." (Quran 2:156)

"Then they got back laden with wealth without any wound or loss of life. If any Muslim dies of grief after all this, he is not to be blamed, but rather there is justification for him before me.

How strange! How strange! By God, my heart sinks to see the unity of these people on their wrong and your dispersion from your right. Woe and grief befall you. You have become the target at which arrows are shot. You are being killed and you do not kill. You are being attacked but you do not attack. God is being disobeyed and you remain agreeable to it.

When I ask you to move against them in summer, you say it is hot weather; spare us till heat subsides from us. When I order you to march in winter, you say it is severely cold; give us time till cold clears from us. These are just excuses for evading heat and cold, because, if you run away from heat and cold, you would be, by God, running away in a greater degree from war.

O' you semblance of men, not men, your intelligence is that of children and your wit is that of the occupants of the curtained canopies (women kept in seclusion from the outside world). I wish I had not seen you, nor known you. By God, this acquaintance has brought about shame and resulted in repentance. May God fight you! You have filled my heart with pus and loaded my bosom with rage. You made me drink mouthfuls of grief, one after the other.

You shattered my counsel by disobeying and leaving me, so much so that Quraysh started saying that the son of Abu Talib is brave but does not know (tactics of) war. God bless them! Is any one of them fiercer in war and older in it than I am? I rose for it, although yet within my twenties, and here I am, having crossed over sixty, but one who is not obeyed can have no opinion.

The Khawarij would later announce that they would be attacking the Alid Caliphate and its army. Though Ali was not of the type to meet violence with violence, this case was different. This was a parasite in Islam that was sucking the life out of the nation and it had to be dealt with straightaway.

"The verdict is for God alone!" In hearing the campaign slogan of the Khawarij, Ali spoke to those in his midst:

A true statement to which a false meaning is intended. It is true that verdict lies but with God, but these people say that the function of governance is only for God. The fact is that there is no escape for men from ruler, good or bad. The faithful persons perform good acts in their rule while the unfaithful enjoy worldly benefits in it.

During rule, God would carry everything to its end. Through the ruler, tax is collected, the enemy is fought, roadways are protected and the right of the weak is taken from the strong, till the virtuous enjoys peace and allowed protection from the oppression of the wicked.

Ali sent Abdullah ibn Abbas to face the leaders of the Khawarij and speak to them before battle would ensue.

Abdullah ibn Abbas met them and asked them directly, "What is your issue of contempt for the Commander of the Faithful?"

"He was a prince to the believers. But when he chose arbitration in the religion of God, he left the faith. So, let him repent after he admits his heresy."

"No believer, who has not a shadow of doubt on his belief, should be expected to deject himself with heresy!"

"He arbitrated."

"God ordered us to arbitrate, even in hunting, so what about in leadership?"

"But the arbitration was forced on him, and he did not accept it."

"Arbitration is like leadership: when the leader is corrupt, it is mandatory to disobey the leader. Similarly, when the arbiter's words contradicted one another, their statements were void..."

Taking to Abdullah ibn Abbas's logic, some of the men began nodding their heads.

Others quickly asserted, "Do not let the rhetoric of Quraysh fool you as proof and evidence against you. For this is from the people whom God described as enemies to be wary of..."

Like that, they evaded a platform for reasonable dialogue and understanding. They did not want to engage in discourse to reach the truth. They assumed that everyone who did not agree with them was a heretic who must be fought and killed. It was not their way or the highway: it was their way or the grave.

They were adamant about going to war with Ali ibn Abi Talib. Thus, Ali met them at the battlefield. But, of course, before he engaged, he spoke to them. The Commander of the Faithful did not enter a battle without speaking to his enemy and placing the burden of proof upon them.

Ali stood before the band of thousands of Khawarij and asked a simple question:

"By God, did you know anyone that was more apprehensive and opposed to this arbitration than me?"

The Khawarij replied, "By God, we did not."

"You know that you coerced me to it until I accepted it?"

"By God, yes we do," they responded.

"Then on what basis do you oppose me and fight me?" he asked them plainly.

"We have committed a grave sin, and for that we repented to God. We ask you to repent to God, and then we will return to you."

"I repent to God for every sin," Ali humbly replied, even though he was the man with no sin whatsoever.

The band of Khawarij lowered their arms and followed Ali. Six thousand men entered into his fold and returned with him to Kufa. When they settled in Kufa, they began spreading a rumor that Ali has retracted his position on the arbitration and saw it as a deviant thing.

"The Commander of the Faithful is waiting for the treasury to be filled and for the resources to be reinforced, and then he will launch his campaign against Syria," they said.

When Ali got wind of this, he spoke to the people in the mosque of Kufa and set the record straight.

"Whoever claimed that I have retracted from the arbitration has lied, and whoever saw it as deviance, then he is more deviant."

The Khawarij left the mosque, shouting, "The verdict is for God alone!"

Those in his company told Ali, "They are revolting against you, O' Commander of the Faithful."

"I will not fight them until they fight me, and they will."

The Khawarij called Ali and his men to the plains of Nahrawan. No matter how much he tried to discourage them from taking up this battle and causing bloodshed, they would not budge. Ali faced them and shared final words with them:

I am warning you that you will be killed on the bend of this canal and on the level of this low area, while you will have no clear excuse before God nor any open authority with you.

You have come out of your houses and then divine decree entangled you.

I had advised you against this arbitration, but you rejected my advice like adversaries and opponents, till I turned my ideas in the direction of your wishes. You are a group whose heads are devoid of wit and intelligence. Woe onto you! I have not put you in any calamity nor wished you harm.

The storm of battle engulfed the plains. The hour of war came and there was no retreat. The armies clashed, but the Commander of the Faithful continued to offer opportunities of repentance. He ordered that the flag of refuge be raised for the opposition.

Abu Ayoub Al-Ansari called out into the battlefield, "Whoever amongst you comes to this flag is safe. Whoever leaves to Iraq is safe. Whoever departs this group from the battlefield is safe. There is no need for bloodshed... you are safe."

Ali commanded his men not to engage in battle unless they were attacked first.

The Khawarij came forward and chanted, "The verdict is for God alone," and "Let us go, let us go to Paradise." They attacked the companions of Ali and the battle ensued. Upon that engagement, Ali himself entered the heart of the battlefield. With his sword and spear he brought annihilation upon them. The battle was swift and victory was for Ali.

Though Ali was fierce with the Khawarij in battle, he showed the utmost kindness and mercy to their orphans and widows. In fact, when he was not in the mosque or the battlefields fending off the treachery of Muawiya after Nahrawan, Ali was seen caring for the families of his enemies with his own hands. As they would curse his name, not knowing who he was, Ali would keep his identity veiled and continue to help them. He brought them food, water, and toys for the children. He gifted rest to the mothers by watching their orphans and cooked for their families. The compassion Ali had for his fellow man was unmatched.

In the end, Ali looked at the Khawarij as a group who had organized and campaigned in their demand for truth. Their problem was they did not know what truth was and their way to get there was ignoble. In this light, they came out against the Imam of their time and dug for themselves a grave fate. They waged war on him, and he defended himself and the Muslims. Only a handful of Khawarij survived. But such a handful would become a ring of assassins and disrupters that vowed to kill Ali, whether it was on or off the battlefield.

CHAPTER 24

THE END OF THE STORM

If you enquire how I am, then listen that I am enduring and strong against the vicissitudes of time.

– Ali

The truce was promised for a year with its conditions. No matter what, Ali refused to break an agreement he entered. That was one of the virtues that distinguished him from the likes of Muawiya.

Ali's caliphate lasted less than five years. In those short years, the Commander of the Faithful faced three civil wars. From the Battle of the Camel and Siffin to the uprising of the Khawarij, and the terrorism of the Umayyads, Ali did not have a day without unrest and turmoil. And yet, he met every day with an unwavering heart, an impeccable mind, and the deepest of faith.

Even after the Battle of Nahrawan, Muawiya would not allow for any days of peace or calm. His aim was to continue a stream of chaos and havoc under the reign of Ali ibn Abi Talib that would make everyone sick and tired of his rule. Though it was not Ali waging these battles and wars, they took place under his watch. Thus, the people would blame him for a rule plagued by civil war, disunity, and strife.

Muawiya continued his assault by sending Dahhak ibn Qays towards Kufa with a unit of four thousand soldiers. The aim of the expedition was to create unrest and havoc in the Kufan metropolitan. He was given orders to attack villages, kill people on the road, pilgrims and non-pilgrims alike, and terrorize the people of Iraq.

Ali would speak to his people about this matter and find them once again lethargic and apathetic in coming to the aid of their countrymen:

> O people, your bodies are together, but your desires are divergent. Your talk softens the hard stones and your action attracts your enemy towards you. You claim in your sittings that you would do this and that, but when fighting approaches, you say to war, "turn thou away" (i.e., flee away). If one calls you for help, the call receives no heed. And he who deals hardly with you, his heart has no solace.

> The excuses are amiss, like those of a debtor unwilling to pay. The ignoble cannot ward off oppression. Right cannot be achieved without effort. Which is the house besides this one to protect? And with which leader (Imam) would you go for fighting after me?

> By God! Deceived is one whom you have deceived while, by God, he who is successful with you receives only useless arrows! You are like broken arrows thrown over the enemy. By God! I am now in the position that I neither confirm your views, nor hope for your support, nor challenge the enemy through you.

What is the matter with you? What is your ailment? What is your cure? The other party is also men of your shape (but they are so different in character). Will there be talk without action, carelessness without piety and greed in things not right?

One of Ali's close companions mobilized an equalizing force of four thousand soldiers to fight off the Umayyads. He desired to crush the enemy at Tadmur, or Palmyra, Syria, but only a minor engagement took place before the Umayyad force retreated.

After Muawiya's commanders had overpowered Ali's officers in Yemen, news came to the Commander of the Faithful. He was disheartened by the lack of readiness and heartiness of his commanders:

I have been informed that Busr has overpowered Yemen. By God, I have begun thinking about these people that they would shortly snatch away the whole country through their unity on their wrong and your disunity from your own right, and separation, your disobedience of your Imam in matters of right and their obedience to their leader in matters of wrong, their fulfilment of the trust in favor of their master and your betrayal, their good work in their cities and your mischief. Even if I give you charge of a wooden bowl, I fear you would run away with its handle.

O My God, they are disgusted of me and I am disgusted of them. They are weary of me and I am weary of them. Change them for me with better ones and change me for them with a worse one. O My God, melt their hearts as salt melts in water. By God, I wish I had only a thousand horsemen of Banu Firas ibn Ghanm, as the poet says:

"If you call them, the horsemen would come to you like the summer cloud."

After defeating the Khawarij at Nahrawan, Ali gave a sermon to his people. He spoke about the annihilation of the Khawarij, the mischief of the Umayyads, and accessing his knowledge:

Praise and eulogy be to God, O people, I have put out the eye of revolt. No one except me advanced towards it when its gloom was swelling and its madness was intense. Ask me before you miss me, because, by God, who has my life in His hands, if you ask me anything between now and the Day of Judgement or about the group who would guide a hundred people and also misguide a hundred people, I would tell you who is announcing its march, who is driving it in the front and who is driving it at the rear, the stages where its riding animals would stop for rest and the final place of stay, and who among them would be killed and who would die a natural death.

When I am dead, hard circumstances and distressing events will befall you, many persons in the position of asking questions will remain silent with cast down eye, while those in the position of replying will lose courage. This will be at a time when wars will descend upon you with all hardship and days will be so hard on you that you would feel them prolonged because of hardship, till God will give victory to those remaining virtuous among you.

When mischiefs come, they confuse right with wrong and when they clear away, they leave a warning. They cannot be known at the time of approach but are recognized at the time of return. They blow like the blowing of winds, striking some cities and missing others.

Beware that the worst mischief for you in my view is the mischief of the Umayyads, because it is blind and also creates darkness. Its sway is general, but its ill effects are for particular people. He who remains clear-sighted in it will be affected by distress, and he who remains blind in it will avoid the distress.

By God, you will find the Umayyads after me worst people for yourselves, like the old unruly she-camel who bites with its mouth, beats with its fore-legs, kicks with its hind legs and refuses to be milked. They would remain over you till they would leave among you only those who benefit them or those who do not harm them.

Their calamity would continue till your seeking help from them would become like the seeking of help by the slave from his master or of the follower from the leader. Their mischief would come to you like evil-eyed fear and pre-Islamic fragments, wherein there would be neither minaret of guidance nor any sign of salvation to be seen.

We, the Household of the Prophet, are free from this mischief, and we are not among those who would engender it.

Thereafter, God would dispel it from you like the removal of the skin (from flesh) through him who would humble them, drag them by necks, make them drink full cups (of hardships), not extend them anything but sword and not clothe them save with fear. At that time, Quraysh would wish at the cost of the world and all its contents to find me even only once and just for the duration of the slaughter of a camel, in order that I may accept from them (the whole of) that of which, at present, I am asking them for only a part, but they are not giving me.

While the Khawarij were defeated and Ali gave this address, Muawiya was sleeping. Muawiya awoke from his slumber to find Abdullah ibn Zubayr at the foot of his bed. Muawiya quickly sat up and asked Abdullah what the purpose of him gazing at his bedside was for.

"O' Muawiya, if you wish for me to be of service to you, I am ready," Abdullah ibn Zubayr said with eagerness.

Looking him in the eye Muawiya responded, "Have you suddenly gained courage, O' Ibn Zubayr?"

"And what of my courage do you doubt, when I stood in the front lines against Ali ibn Abi Talib?" Zubayr responded defensively.

"Ali defeated you and your father with his left hand, while he kept his right-hand open challenging anyone to come forward and fight him…"

Muawiya could not challenge such bravery. No one could. Thus, he resorted to all the lowly tactics he utilized to take the war away from traditional battle of man-to-man combat. It became a war that abducted the hearts and minds, and deflated the rigor of fighting against injustice by those loyal to the caliphate.

Ali's face turned away from war with Muawiya, not because he did not have the stomach for it, but because he became a commander without an army. Muawiya's heart danced in joy as his schemes to weaken the stronghold of Ali worked. The bribery, blackmail, terrorism, and mischief he played for years saw its fruition.

Some saw this as a show of Muawiya's military prowess and political astuteness, compared to Ali's disunited and brittle military and political condition. But it could not be farther from the truth. Ali's objectives were different than Muawiya's. Muawiya achieved his aims through his conniving means. Ali also achieved his goals, which were in part to demonstrate the correct means to achieving one's aims. Ali ibn Abi Talib established the standard of just governance for people to see across the centuries. To compare those before him and those that would come after him, Ali set the standard.

He made it clear, even in the time of war and sedition, how Muslims are to engage with one another, regardless of which side of the conflict they may be on. Ali demonstrated the rules of engagement and the rules of warfare with poetic eloquence. Those civil wars were not a point of weakness on Ali's legacy, they were a reality that he dealt with in the greatest degree of ethics and humanity. Muawiya may have gotten his share of jewels, but Ali would always be the lens by which to tell of true value and worth.

The sheer hatred Muawiya had for Ali was beyond explanation. He ordered his officials and agents to scour the lands for the followers of Ali and persecute them.

"Eliminate them from their homes, and strip them of their sustenance..." he told his men.

Anyone accused of being a follower of Ali was beaten and their home destroyed before their eyes.

When Abdullah ibn Abbas celebrated a new baby boy, Muawiya congratulated him and asked him of his name.

Abdullah smiled and said, "I named him Ali and gave him the title of Abul Hasan."

Muawiya turned red. Unable to control his anger, he screamed in Abdullah's face.

"No! No! You cannot combine both the name and that title at once! Change one of them at least!"

The blind hatred the Umayyads had for Ali was seen on all levels. Muawiya's hatred drove him to use state funds from the Muslim treasury to promote his own handpicked preachers. One of them was Samra ibn Jundub. Muawiya gave him four hundred thousand dirhams to preach to the people of Damascus with specific interpretations of the Holy Quran.

Among the people is he whose talk about worldly life impresses you, and he holds God witness to what is in his heart, though he is the staunchest of enemies. If he were to wield authority, he would try to cause corruption in the land and to ruin the crop and the stock, and God does not like corruption.

Samra told the people that the aforementioned verse was describing Ali ibn Abi Talib.

"And among the people is he who sells his soul seeking the pleasure of God, and God is most kind to [His] servants." Samra would then assert that this verse would describe Abd al-Rahman ibn Muljam – a man who would do unspeakable things.

Muawiya funded the promotion of pseudo-scholars like Abu Huraira, Amr ibn Al-Aas, and Al-Mugheera ibn Shu'ba. Amr, for example, falsely narrated that the Prophet said, "The Household of Abu Talib are not vicegerents of mine, rather the vicegerents of God are the virtuous believers."

Yet, with all of their attempts to tarnish his name and legacy, Ali is untouchable. He is that beaming light that brightens the path for any seeker of truth, for how could he not be, when he is truth itself? Ali's reality was so undeniable that even Muawiya felt the vacuum of his loss.

When Muawiya would be informed of Ali's death, he said, "All of knowledge and jurisprudence has gone with the death of the son of Abu Talib."

Bewildered and concerned, Muawiya's brother, 'Utba, turned to him and warned, "Make sure the people of Syria do not hear this from you."

"Leave me be!" Muawiya waved his brother away.

Even Muawiya could not deny the loss of Ali when it came to his position in knowledge and faith. All the scholars of Islam, contemporary to Ali and after him, would trace their knowledge back to Ali. There was simply no doubt in the matter. Though Muawiya unleashed a propaganda machine to tarnish his name, he still waited for Ali to take the true meaning of things that mattered most.

With all the tribulation and turmoil Ali faced, one would suppose that grief and submission would be the natural course. But Ali submitted to nothing short of the glory of God. He described his state of mind quite beautifully in a letter he sent to his brother, Aqeel ibn Abi Talib. In part he states:

As for your enquiry about my opinion on fighting, I am in favor of fighting those who regard fighting as lawful until I die. The abundance of men around me does not increase me in strength, nor does their dispersal from me cause any loneliness.

Surely, do not consider the son of your father as being weak or afraid, even though all people have forsaken him, or bowing down submissively before injustice or handing over his reins into the hand of the puller, or allowing his back to be used by the rider to sit upon. But he is as the man of Banu Salim has said:

'If you enquire how I am, then listen that I am enduring and strong against the vicissitudes of time.'

Ali stood the test of time. He did not waiver with the lack of friends and supporters. Ali challenged the day, every day. He met life with a vigor for his cause that very few in history could claim. Those who live in honor often strive to die in the same manner. If anyone in history shared glory in both life and death, it was Ali ibn Abi Talib.

CHAPTER 25

TO MY SON

By the Lord of the Kaaba, I have won.

– Ali

Ali's life was cut short by the hands of the Khawarij and the reach of the Umayyads. There was not a more poetic way for this legend to leave this world but in the state that he loved most – kneeling before his Lord in prayer. For if anyone were to take the life of Ali, it could not be on the battlefield. There was no earthly match for him. He had to be in a state of complete detachment from the realm of mortals.

Ali would rise before dawn to meet Almighty God. He entered the mosque of Kufa, where he led prayer, met with his companions, and ruled in the court of law. Kufa was his home and the capital of his reign, a reign he established only to bring glory to God. As dawn broke, Ali made the call to prayer and woke those who lay asleep in the house of God.

As he walked by those in slumber, he noticed one particular man lying flat on his stomach. He paused. The man was not asleep. He hid something. An intention and an objective. But this could not be hidden from the vicegerent of God. Ali knew him and knew his motive.

"Rise from the sleep of the Devil," he advised him. Indeed, sleeping on one's stomach was abhorred by prophetic tradition. Yet, perhaps Ali's admonition of the man was beyond mere advice on piety and more so a message to his assailant that he knew who he was and what he was about to do.

The man's name was Abd al-Rahman ibn Muljam, who, only moments later, would be the man history would record as the killer of the Prophet's disciple.

Ali would proceed to begin his prayers. He would call onto God's greatest name. He praised Him. Ali kneeled. Ali prostrated. Ali would rise again.

Abd al-Rahman crept up behind the other believers in prayer. He moved stealthily between the lines of men worshiping their Creator. His heart thumping, brow sweating, he leaped at his moment. Ali was rising from prostration, not yet complete in his prayer. Abd al-Rahman took his poison-dipped dagger and struck Ali ibn Abi Talib on his head.

Upon that strike, Ali called out to his Lord in words that no man had used before:

By the Lord of the Kaaba, I have won.

He won the pleasure of his Lord and his Prophet. He won the title of truth and its infinite legacy. He won honor and glory greater than the sum of all men. He won.

The people leaped at Abd al-Rahman and nearly tore him to shreds. The Commander of the Faithful's sons came to his aid and held their father tightly – a sight that ripped even the hardest of hearts to shreds. The people that got hold of the assassin were on the verge of killing him. Ali ordered that they stop and that he be treated justly. He was not to be tortured, and only an equivalent punishment should be given to him. It is said that Ali even instructed his men to give the assassin water and to loosen the ropes around his wrists.

Ali had no vengeance, save for the glory of God. He showed mercy, not only to those who fought him in battle, but even to the man who would fatally injure him. Due to the severity of his wound, Ali died within days of the attempt on his life. It is a feat that Ali could not be killed on the battlefield by any man, and that the only way his life could be taken was while he kneeled in prayer. The prayer-mat was Ali's sanctuary. It was the position in which he most loved to be. His sons relay hearing their father, Ali, whispering to God in his prayers:

> My Lord, I do not worship you out of fear, nor do I worship you out of greed. I worship you as I found you worthy of worship.

Ali knew his Lord better than any man. And he knew Him, because he knew himself. "Whoever knows himself will know his Lord," Ali repeated to his companions.

Before he died, Ali wrote a letter to his eldest son, Hasan. In part, the letter advises his son on life, society, and success. The words of wisdom that he held for his son rippled into the centuries for generations to come. They serve as a compass on how to live life to its fullest, and how to attain our glorious destiny as servants of God. Ali spoke to his son, and all sons – both of his time and all of time:

> From the father who is soon to die, who acknowledges the hardships of the times, who has turned away from life, who has submitted himself to the calamities of time, who realizes the evils of the world, who is living in the abodes of the dead and is due to depart from them any day; to the son who yearns for what is not to be achieved, who is treading the path of those who have died, who is the victim of ailments, who is entangled in the worries of the days, who is a target of hardships, a slave of the world, a trader of its deception, a debtor of wishes, a prisoner of mortality, an ally of worries, a neighbor of grief, a victim of distresses, who has been over-powered by desires, and who is a successor of the dead.

> Now you should know that what I have learnt from the turning away of this world from me, the onslaught of time over me and the advancing of the next world towards me is enough to prevent me from remembering anyone except myself, and from thinking beyond myself. But when I confined myself to my own worries, leaving the worries of others, my intelligence saved me and protected me from my desires. It clarified to me my affairs and led me to seriousness wherein there was no trickery and truth which was not tarnished by falsehood. Here, I found you a part of myself, rather I found you my whole, so much so that if anything befell you, it was as though it befell me and if death came to you, it was as though it came to me. Consequently, your affairs meant to me what my own matters meant to me. So, I have

written this piece of advice to you as an instrument of seeking help through it, whether I remain alive for you or cease to exist.

I advise you to fear God, O my child, abide by His commands, fill your heart with remembrance of Him and cling to hope from Him. No connection is more reliable than the connection between you and God, provided you take hold of it. Enliven your heart with preaching, kill it by denial, energize it with firm belief, enlighten it with wisdom, humiliate it by recalling death, make it believe in mortality, make it see the misfortunate of this world, make it fear the authority of the time and the severity of some changes during the nights and the days, place before it the events of past people, recall to it what befell those who were before you and walk among their cities and ruins, then see what they did and from what they have gone away and where they have gone and stayed. You will find that they departed from their friends and remain in loneliness. Shortly, you too will be like one of them. Therefore, plan for your place of stay and do not sell your next life with this world.

O my son, when I noticed I was of goodly age and noticed I was increasing in weakness, I hastened with my will for you and wrote down prominent points of it, in case death overtook me before I divulged to you what I have in my heart, or in case my wit be affected as my body has been affected, or forces of passions or mischief of the world overtake you, making you like a stubborn camel. Certainly, the heart of a young man is like uncultivated land. It accepts whatever is strewn on it. So, I hastened to mold you properly before your heart hardened up and your mind became occupied, so you might be ready to accept through your intelligence the results of the experience of others and be saved from going through these experiences yourself. In this way, you would avoid the hardship of seeking them and the difficulties of experimenting. Thus, you are getting to know what we had experienced and even those things are becoming clear to you which we might have missed.

O my son, even though I have not reached the age which those before me have, I looked into their behavior and thought over events of their lives. I walked among their ruins till I was as one of them. In fact, by virtue of those, of their affairs that have become known to me, it is as though I have lived with them from the first to the last. I have therefore been able to discern the impure from the clean and the benefit from the harm.

I have selected for you the choicest of those matters and collected for you their good points and have kept away from you their useless points. Since I feel for your affairs as a living father should feel and I aim at giving you training, I thought it should be at a time when you are advancing in age and new on the stage of the world, possessing upright intention and clean heart and that I should begin with the teaching of the Book of God, and its interpretation, the laws of Islam and its commands, its lawful matters and unlawful matters and that I should not go beyond these for you. Then I feared, lest you should get confused, as other people had been confused, on account of their passions and different views. Therefore, in spite of my dislike for you being so warned, I thought it better for me to make this position strong, rather than leave you in a position where I do not regard you safe from falling into destruction. I hoped that God would help you in your straightforwardness and guide you in your resoluteness. Consequently, I wrote this piece of my will for you.

Know, my son, what I love most for you to adopt from my will is to fear God, to confine yourself to what God has made obligatory on you, and to follow the actions of your forefathers and the virtuous people of your household, because they did not fall short in seeing for themselves what you will see for yourself, and they went about their affairs as you would like to think about your affairs. Thereafter, their thinking led them to discharge the obligations they came to know of and to desist from what they were not required to do. If your heart does not accept this without acquiring knowledge as they acquired it, then your search should first be by way of understanding and learning and not by falling into doubts or getting entangled in quarrels.

And before you probe into this, you should begin by seeking Allah's help and turning to Him for competence and keeping aloof from everything that throws you into doubt or flings you towards misguidance. When you have made sure that your heart is clean and humble, your thoughts have come together and you have only one thought, which is about this matter, then you will see what I have explained to you; but if you have not been able to achieve that peace of observation and thinking which you would like to have, then know that you are only stamping the ground like a blind she-camel and falling into darkness, while a seeker of religion should not grope in the dark or create confusion. It is better to avoid this.

Appreciate my advice, O my son, and know He who is the Master of death is also the Master of life, that the Creator causes death as well; that He who destroys is also the restorer of life and that He who inflicts disease is also the curer. This world continues in the way Allah has made it with regard to its pleasures, trials, rewards on the Day of Judgement, and all that He wishes and you do not know. If anything of this advice is not understood by you, then attribute it to your ignorance of it, because when you were first born, you were born ignorant. Thereafter, you acquired knowledge. There are many matters of which you are ignorant and in which your sight first wonders and your eye wanders, then after this you see them. Therefore, cling to Him who created you, fed you and put you in order. Your worship should be for Him, your eagerness should be towards Him and your fear should be of Him."

Ali's words would eternally be etched in the souls of truth-seekers and the lovers of light.

Dear world, go and fool someone other than me. You will not stand a chance with me.

His words forever ring true. Muawiya and his likes had this world, and the world had them. But for Ali, he was never interested in that game of power and lust – one that crumbled nations and kingdoms. He had no desire, nor appetite for it. Ali was above such things. He gave everything he had for the salvation of the faithful and the oppressed – in the service of the Prophet and for the love of God. Had people only realized this love, things may have been different. The Prophet had once said to his cousin, Abdullah ibn Abbas something profound:

If only people would unite in the love of Ali ibn Abi Talib, God would have not created Hellfire.

Ali radiated a light that would forever serve as a compass for humanity – illuminating through the legacy of the eleven princes that followed from his lineage. Today we are warmed by the radiating rays and the luminous light of the twelfth prince, the Master of Time and the Awaited Savior – the Mahdi. Perhaps the elixir of love will be manifested again through him. Until then, the lovers of Ali remain patient, for in their hearts is a secret prayer that saves them in every moment of difficulty:

Call upon Ali, the revealer of wonders
He will be your helper in hardships
Every anxiety and sorrow will end
Through your guardianship
O' Ali! O' Ali! O' Ali!

Whether they chanted his name by the thousands, or stood against him, just the same, Ali was unblemished. His immaculate name echoes in the valleys of eternity. Ali was the manifestation of Muhammad's truth. He was the standard of justice and the embodiment of grace. He cannot be compared justly to those who challenged him. That world of power and lust never stood a chance against Ali. Always above the fray, Ali remained... an immaculate dream, sadly unrealized and untapped by the people in his midst. They could not realize his splendor and embrace his endless love. But the few who truly pursued love and light, they knew that Ali was their answer. Then and now, across the basins of time, Ali will forever be... the Elixir of Love.

SELECT BIBLIOGRAPHY

The primary sources from which the details of this narrative were derived are found in the cited list below. Many of these sources were retrieved through the original work of the late Sayyid Muhammad Bahreluloum, *Fi Rihab A'immat Ahlulbayt: Al-Imam Ali*. That work, along with the accompanying sources below, were researched and used in their original Arabic language, unless otherwise indicated.

Abbas, Hassan. *The Prophet's Heir: The Life of Ali ibn Abi Talib* (London: Yale University Press, 2021).

Abd Rabbih, Ahmad ibn Muhammad ibn. *al-'Iqd al-Farīd*. (Beirut: Dār al-Kitāb al-'Arabī, 1993).

Al-Akkad, Abbas Mahmoud. *'Abqariyet al-Imam* (Cairo: Nahdet Masr, 2003).

Amini, Abd al-Husayn. *Al-Ghadir fi al-Kitab wa al-Sunnah wa al-Adab*, 11 vols (Beirut: Dar al-Kutub al-Arabi, 1967).

Al-Asfahani, Abu al-Faraj. *Maqātil al-Ṭālibiyyīn* (Beirut: Mu'assisa al-'A'lami li-l-Matbu'at, 1965).

Al-Asfahani, Abu Na'eem. *Hiliyat al-Awliya'* (Cairo: 1932).

Al-'Askari, Sayyid Murtadha. *Ahadeeth Umm al-Mu'mineen Aisha* (Beirut: Al-Ghadeer, 1997).

Al-Atheer, Ali Ibn. *Usd al-Ghabah fi Marifat al-Saḥabah* (Beirut: Dar Ibn Hazm, 2012).

Al-Atheer, Ali Ibn. *Al-Kamil fi al-Tareekh* (Beirut: Dar al-Kutub al-'Ilmiya, 1987).

Bahreluloom, Sayyid Muhammad. *Fi Rihab A'immat Ahlulbayt: Al-Imam Ameer al-Mu'mineen Ali.* (Beirut: Dar al-Zahra, 1980).

Al-Balādhurī, ʾAḥmad ibn Yaḥyā ibn Jabir. *Ansab al-Ashraf* (Beirut: Yutlabu Min F. Shataynir, 1978).

Chamseddine, Muhammad Mehdi. *Hussain's Revolution* (Detroit, The Mainstay Foundation, 2016).

Charafeddine, Sayyid Sadreddine. *Haleef Makhzoum: Ammar ibn Yasser* (Beirut: Dar al-Adwa', 1992).

Chirri, Mohammad Jawad. *The Brother of the Prophet Mohammad*, vols I and II, revised edn. (Detroit: The Islamic Center of America, 1988).

Al-Hadid, Izz al-Din ibn Abi. *Sharh Nahj al-Balagha*, ed. Muhammad Abu al-Fadl Ibrahim (Cairo: Isa al-Babi al-Halabi, 1959).

Al-Hindi, al-Muttaqi. *Kanz al-Ummal Fee Sunan al-Aqwal wa al-Af'al*, ed. Mahmud Umar al-Dumyati (Beirut: Dār al-Kutub al-'Ilmīyah, 1998).

Hisham, Abu Muhammad Abdul Malik ibn. *Al-Seerah al-Nabawiyya* (Beirut: Dar al-Ma'rifa, 1982).

Hussein, Taha. *Al-Ftina al-Kubra* (Beirut: Dar al-Maaref, 2007)

Ibn Kathir. *Al-Sira Al-Nabawiyyah: The Life of the Prophet Muhammad*, Vol. 1, trans. by Professor Trevor Le Gassick (London: Garnet Publishers, 1998).

Khalid, Khalid Muhammad. *Fi Rihab Ali* (Beirut: Dar al-Maaref, 2005).

Al-Khwārizmī, Muḥammad ibn Mūsā. *Manāqib Amīr al-Muʾminīn*, ed. Malik Mahmudi (Qom: Jami'a Mudarresin).

Al-Irbilī, ʿAlī ibn ʿIsā. *Kashf al-Ghumma fī Maʿrifat al-Aʾimma* (Beirut: Dār al-Aḍwāʾ, 1985).

Jordac, George. *The Voice of Human Justice*, 2nd edn, trans. M. Fazal Haq (Qom: Ansariyan Publications, 2007).

Al-Juwayni, Sadr al-Din Ibrahim. *Farāʾid al-Simṭayn fī Faḍāʾil al-Murtaḍā wa l-Batūl wa l-Sibṭayn wa l-Aʾimma min Dhurrīyyatihim ʿAlayhim al-Salām* (Beirut: Al-Mahmudi institute, 1980).

Al-Marwazī, Abd-Allāh ibn Muslim ibn Qutayba al-Dīnawarī. *Al-Imama w Al-Siyasa (Tarikh al-Khulafa)*, ed. Zini Taha (Cairo: Muʾassasat al-Halabi, 1967)

Al-Mudhaffar, Muhammad Ridha. *Al-Saqeefa* (Qom: Ansariyan Publiations, 1995).

Al-Mufid, Shaykh. *Kitab Al-Irshad* (Beirut: Dar al-Mufid, 1993).

Muzahim, Nasr ibn. *Waq'at Ṣiffin.* (Qom: Ayatollah Najafi Mar'ashi Library, 1982).

Al-Nasai, Ahmad ibn Shu'ayb. *Khasa'is Amir al-Mu'minin Ali ibn Abi Talib* (Qom: Bustan-e Ketab, 2003).

Al-Nesapuri, Al-Hakim. *Al-Mustadrak ala aṣ-Ṣaheehayn* (Beirut: Dar al-Ma'rifa, 1970).

Al-Qarashi, Baqir Sharif. *The Life of Imam Ali Ibn Abi-Talib,* trans. Badr Shahin (Qom: Ansariyan Publications, 2010).

Al-Qunduzi, Sulayman ibn Ibrahim. *Yanābī' al-mawadda lī-dhawī l-qūrbā* (Beirut: Mu'assisa al-'A'lami li-l-Matbu'at, 1997).

Radi, Sharif. *Nahj al-Balagha,* trans. Sayed Ali Reza as *The Peak of Eloquence* (New York, 1996).

Razwy, Syed A.A. *Khadija-tul Kubra (The Wife of Prophet Mohammad): A Short Story of Her Life* (New York: Tehrike Tarsile Quran, Inc., 1990).

Saad, Muhammad ibn. *Al-Tabaqat al-Kubra* (Cairo: Dar Ibn al-Jawzi, 1994).

Shahr Ashub, Muhammad ibn Ali ibn. *Manāqib Āl Abī Ṭālib* (Qom: 'Allama Publications, 1980).

Al-Shiblanj, Mu'min ibn Hasan. *Nour al-Absar* (Qom: Radi Publishing, 1982).

Al-Tabari, Abu Jafar Muhammad ibn Jarir. *Tareekh al-Rusul wa al-Mulook,* translated as *The History of al-Tabari,* Vol. 15, "The Crisis of the Early Caliphate: The Reign of Uthman, A.D. 644-656/A.H. 24-35", trans. R. Stephen Humphreys (Albany: State University of New York Press, 1990).

Al-Tabari, Abu Jafar Muhammad ibn Jarir. *Tareekh al-Rusul wa al-Mulook,* translated as *The History of al-Tabari,* Vol. 16. "The Community Divided: The Caliphate of Ali. A.D. 656-657/A.H. 35-36", trans. Adrian Brockett (Albany: State University of New York Press, 1997).

Al-Tabari, Abu Jafar Muhammad ibn Jarir. *Tareekh al-Rusul wa al-Mulook,* translated as *The History of al-Tabari,* Vol. 17, "The First Civil War: From the battle of Siffin to the Death of Ali, A.D. 656-661/A.H. 36-40", trans. G.R. Hawting (Albany: State University of New York Press, 1996).

Al-Ya'qubi, Ahmad ibn Wadhih. *The Works of Ibne Wadih Al-Yaqubi: The History (Tarikh) – The Rise of Islam to the Reign of al-Mutamid,* ed. Matthew Gordon, Chase F. Robinson, Everett K. Rowson and Michael Fishbein, Vol. 3 (Leiden: Brill, 2018).

Printed in Great Britain
by Amazon